TACTICS

For Simm, Sally and Sosha

And success

[signature]

JAN ZUCHOWSKI

TACTICS

**10 SUCCESS
STRATEGIES FOR
YOUNG PROFESSIONALS**

CONNECTIONS
BOOK PUBLISHING

A CONNECTIONS EDITION
This edition published in Great Britain in 2011 by
Connections Book Publishing Limited
St Chad's House, 148 King's Cross Road, London WC1X 9DH
www.connections-publishing.com

British Library Cataloguing-in-Publication data available on request.

ISBN 978-1-85906-341-5

10 9 8 7 6 5 4 3 2 1

Phototypeset in MetaPlus and Helvetica Neue using InDesign on Apple Macintosh
Printed in Singapore

CONTENTS

INTRODUCTION 7

TACTIC 1
DECIDE WHAT YOU WANT 13
   Exercise WHAT'S IMPORTANT TO YOU? 15
   Exercise EXPAND YOUR VISION 20
   Exercise CREATIVE VISUALIZATION 22
   Tactics in Action REHEARSING SUCCESS IN YOUR MIND 25

TACTIC 2
WALK THE WALK 27
   Tactics in Action AN EPIC DREAM 30
   Exercise GET UNDER THEIR SKIN 32
   Exercise MAKING GREAT DECISIONS 36

TACTIC 3
CONFRONT YOUR FEARS 42
   Exercise IT'S A QUESTION OF SIZE 45
   Exercise ASSESS THE FACTS 48
   Tactics in Action MY TURNING POINT 51
   Exercise FOCUS YOUR ENERGY 53

TACTIC 4
UNDERSTAND POWER 56
   Exercise EXPAND YOUR THINKING 60
   Tactics in Action THE MAN WHO SELLS DREAMS 65

TACTIC 5
PRACTISE PERSUASION 69
   Exercise READING THE SIGNS 75
   Tactics In Action PAYING ATTENTION PAYS OFF 77
   Exercise NINE-STEP PERSUASION STRATEGY 81

TACTIC 6
USE SMART THINKING   82
    Exercise NEGOTIATION   84
    Tactics in Action THE MERGER   89
    Negotiation answers   95

TACTIC 7
BUILD YOUR TEAMS   99
    Tactics in Action PERFORMANCE WITH A PURPOSE   106
    Exercise SHIFT YOUR BELIEFS   109

TACTIC 8
INSPIRE CONFIDENCE   112
    Exercise THE BIGGER YOU   115
    Tactics in Action INSPIRE RESULTS AND HAVE FUN   119
    Tactics in Action SHARE VALUES, BELIEFS AND DREAMS   125

TACTIC 9
COMMUNICATE FOR RESULTS   126
    Tactics in Action WHAT DO THEY NEED TO KNOW?   130
    Exercise DISCOVER SECRETS PEOPLE GIVE AWAY   133
    Exercise ASSESS YOUR PERFORMANCE   136

TACTIC 10
COMMIT TO CHANGE   140
    Tactics in Action THE 'EUREKA' MOMENT   145
    Exercise THE FOUR-STEP EXERCISE   147

WHAT NEXT?   150
    Exercise TAKE YOUR OWN ADVICE   152

Resources   157
The author   159
Acknowledgements   160

INTRODUCTION

You will have more than 50,000 thoughts today,
so you might as well make them big ones.

DONALD TRUMP

Upgrade your life

Success is never an accident. It is something you create. It is something YOU do.

Whatever you achieve is an outcome of the thoughts and attitudes you have and the actions that you take with a focused sense of purpose. Isn't it reasonable to think, therefore, that if you know the actions you need to take, and the attitudes and beliefs you need to have, and if you apply those actions, attitudes and beliefs consistently, you will be more than likely to arrive at where you want to be?

In this book I want to prove that YOU have the power to bring about the changes in YOUR life that you are seeking ... and that you CAN transform your future.

Wherever you are in life – whether you are happy and satisfied, or if you are frustrated and disillusioned – you have arrived here because of the thoughts you have had and the actions you have taken. You are the person you have made. So if you have done it once, you can do it again – only better this time.

I remember very clearly the day a billionaire whose achievements I admire said to me, 'You have the exact amount of success you deserve.' At the time I was taken aback; I was offended. I felt as if a bucket of ice-cold water had just been hurled over me. My own view was that I thought I deserved rather more success than seemed to be coming my way.

After the initial shock had worn off, however, there dawned on me an earth-shaking realization. I began to understand that I had to change, to start taking responsibility for my own achievements. Whatever I wanted, I would have to bring about myself: nobody else was going to do it for me. What I created, I would have; what I failed to create, I would not have.

I began to understand that successful people do things in certain ways. So, if I wanted to join their ranks, I would need to make some radical shifts, both in how I thought and in the way I operated. Either I chose to do things as successful people did them, or I didn't. It was up to me.

The start of your incredible journey

In this book we will investigate the different elements that can accelerate your success as well as exploring what you need to do in order to create the life that you want. Some parts may not make comfortable reading. However, success is not created by being comfortable.

I'm proposing we take a journey together. It's a journey through the processes of discovering the thoughts and attitudes you will need to develop in order to create what you want at your next level of achievement and beyond. This journey is about action. We are going to work on strategies that, if you implement them, will transform who you are, and will unleash your potential for an inspired life, a life that will impact significantly – and beneficially – on yourself and on the world around you.

Together, we will look at what is genuinely important to you, at what would convince you that you are living your life 'with meaning'. We'll consider what might be stopping you from taking action in the direction of your dreams, and we'll work out how to overcome it. We'll explore what you can do to enhance your communication skills, to inspire confidence and trust in those around you, and to emerge as a natural leader. You will learn how to bring out the best in other people, and so enhance the quality of their lives, too.

As we start, it is very important to keep one thing in mind: you are embarking on a process that can change your life, and change needs time and attention. So be sure to GIVE it time. Take time out of your busy schedule to make the strategies on which we are going to work part of your daily routines. If you make and take the time, you will astonish yourself with what you can achieve.

> *Don't say you don't have enough time. You have exactly the same number of hours per day that were given to Helen Keller, Louis Pasteur, Michelangelo, Mother Teresa, Leonardo da Vinci, Thomas Jefferson and Albert Einstein.*
>
> H. Jackson Brown Jr, *Life's Little Instruction Book*

The choices you make as you go about your hours and days accumulate to shape your future. The quality of your choices determines the quality of the journey you make through your life.

Taking control

A long time ago, I made the decision that, if life is a journey, the mode of travel I prefer is first class. I concluded that I am willing to do whatever it takes to make that possible. This was a defining moment for me because it became the benchmark for what I now do each day.

I learned to be constantly aware that each choice has a consequence. I now understand that I have control over how I elect to travel the life I have mapped out. I exercise that control by picking options daily that are in line with what I want. Early on I resolved that when I come to the end of my days I want to be able to look back on my life and say, 'Wow! What a ride!' – and I made the decision to be willing to take responsibility for making that happen.

I've written this book in the hope that for you, too, the time has now come to redesign your future. Consider what you want to create for yourself and for others. How are you going to impact on the world? How will future generations know that you have walked this earth?

I am always curious about how super-achievers go about creating their success, how they join up different thoughts that translate into powerful action, how they constantly reinvent themselves in order to grow and to keep on growing. What is it they do when they make their mark on the world? Some people look at a situation and see a challenging situation, perhaps something to be feared. Others look at exactly the same thing and see 'Opportunity' flashing brightly overhead. Which response will you choose?

How to use this book

I hope this book will inspire you. Even more, I hope it will help you change your life. I have deliberately made it a PRACTICAL book, reflecting a highly PRACTICAL approach you can take to your future.

It is built around ten personal 'tactics' – tactics you will use to transform your life. As you work through each of the ten tactics, you will discover that there are three threads running through them all, supporting and reinforcing each other. These vital threads are: what you think, what you do, and how you interact with other people. Together they will shape the results that you achieve.

By understanding how the processes work, you can adjust your own approaches to your life, to create a better, more rewarding future for yourself and for those around you.

Work through the tactics in sequence. Each one builds on the skills and ways of thinking you have learned in the previous one. Take time to mull over the questions: think about how they relate to your life and explore what could be possible for you. Give everything that you do your all. This is a defining moment for you. How much effort you put into our work together will determine the quality of the results you will obtain. You are standing on the threshold of a remarkable future ... and you have to be willing to step through that doorway and do whatever it takes.

We are going to look at how elite performers approach what they do – because with practice you can do it too. People who are at the top of their game have refined how they think and what they do in order to achieve their results. Make the decision that you belong among them, and that you are willing to reshape your thinking and routines to make that possible.

Your new ways of thinking will foster new forms of behaviour and habits that take you closer to your objectives more quickly. As you expand your awareness of possibility, you will leave behind attitudes and activities that you will realize have been holding you back. You will find yourself becoming ever more capable of taking direct personal responsibility for your results.

You will also discover how the success that you want can come from and through other people. Others can bring magic and opportunities into your life, if you make it possible for them to do so. The quality of your communications and your relationships needs to be such that it creates a rich environment of empowerment and possibility both for yourself and for others.

You must be ready and willing to bring magic and opportunities into other people's lives to help them build their own dreams and aspirations – and to do it first! It doesn't work like a cash transaction, but you will find that, as you create the energy of success and achievement for those around you, it will start to come back to you, too.

Your journal

An important tool for you to use in our work together is your journal. Purchase a top-quality notebook for this purpose – one you feel proud to own – and every morning spend twenty minutes writing in it. Write about your thoughts, what motivates you, where you are heading, your hopes and plans ... indeed, whatever feels right for you at that moment. Think of it as a daily letter to yourself. You shouldn't let anyone else see this. Your journal is your own private discourse, a place where you can work through your ideas and let them grow.

The value to you of writing in your journal lies in the process of writing itself. When writing by hand, you focus and sharpen up your active thinking in a way you cannot do by thinking alone. When you think things through ordinarily, you use the conscious, critical part of your mind. When you write by hand, the physical activity of forming the words transmits your thoughts to the unconscious part of your mind. Your unconscious mind is alerted to what is important to you and then, as you go about your business of the day, somewhere deep inside these thoughts intermingle, new connections are made and you will find yourself noticing things that you would not have noticed before. It's where creative thinking happens at its best.

This is not a time to be working out how you are going to get your car to the garage for a service or what the dinner arrangements are for that evening. No, this is a time reserved for you to work on the life you are creating, and for you to build your dreams.

The future you

Prepare to build big dreams. Many people haven't allowed themselves to dream exciting dreams for so long that they have forgotten how. At first you may need to think just a bit more expansively than you had previously dared; then push a bit more. How close to the edge dare you step? How far could your dreams go if you didn't restrict them in any way? If you cannot dream something, you can be pretty sure you won't do it. I often ask myself the question, 'Is this as big a dream as Richard Branson or Barack Obama or Donald Trump or Mahatma Gandhi might have had?'

Our work together is designed to ensure that you obtain the best possible value from the unique combination of factors that combine to make you *you*: your talents, your skills, your abilities, your interests – and your dreams! Make a commitment to yourself now that you will work through the exercises in this book and on the accompanying website www.tactics4talent.com and take your success to the level you deserve. Your time has come.

TACTIC 1
DECIDE WHAT YOU WANT

The mind, once expanded to the dimensions of larger ideas,
never returns to its original size.

OLIVER WENDELL HOLMES

Who are you? Where do you belong?

Let's start by looking at what is going on for you at present. Perhaps you find yourself at a stage where it seems that life should simply be more rewarding, more inspired, more fun? Maybe you are quite successful already, but feel that you need a breakthrough to lead you to some greater achievements? Perhaps you have become aware of a gnawing discomfort deep inside, suggesting to you that you could be more, do more and have more if only you knew how. These are all powerful feelings because together they form a strong starting point from which to create the future that you really want: a life that you live through choice.

In this first tactic we are going to investigate how you have arrived at this point and where you might be heading. We will also explore what other ways there might be of looking at your future plans. It's important to acknowledge that you haven't arrived at where you are by accident. You have arrived here as a direct result of the thoughts you have had up until now, the choices you have made and the actions you have taken.

That's okay. What's in the past is in the past. Leave it there. You now have the opportunity to build bridges to a future that you design with a new level of awareness. If you start thinking differently, your thoughts will lead to actions that you might not otherwise take, and will reshape the sort of person you become. The nature of the choices you make will change; the nature of your results will change. It's a magnificently empowering position to be in, since you begin to redefine everything that might be possible.

Because designing a new future means thinking things you hadn't thought before, you need to be willing to step outside your comfort zone a little. Be bold! Think adventure, think fun, think vitality, passion and energy. It's likely that very soon you will begin to feel that concepts such as 'average' or 'ordinary' are no longer acceptable to you. You will become increasingly aware of how elite players think and what they do. More than likely, you will start to develop a hunger to join their ranks, too.

▶ PAGE 17

EXERCISE **WHAT'S IMPORTANT TO YOU?**

Work through these steps in your journal (see page 11).

1. Make a list of what is important to you in all of the different aspects of your life – your career or business, your relationships, your finances, your physical and mental fitness, your spirituality ... We call these your values. Limit your list to ten to twelve values in all: if you list more you will find you are dealing with peripherals. Leave plenty of space between each one so that you can make notes. If you are stuck for thoughts, the keywords in the box on page 16 offer some suggestions on the sort of things you might think about.

2. How do you know that the values you have identified are important to you? What are you doing in your day-to-day life that tells you they are important? Make a note about what you notice for each one. If you believe that developing your career is important to you, for example, or your goal is maintaining a fit body, finding a partner, travelling ... but you aren't actually doing anything about it, ask yourself if it is really important to you. Does it actually belong among your values after all? That can change in the future, of course, but for now we are looking at your present reality.

3. Say WHY each value is important to you. A good phrase to use is 'It means that ...' For example, 'X is important to me because it means that I could ...' It's a useful way for you to test for yourself whether something is as important to you as you think it is. As you complete this section of the exercise, you may find a sense of awareness beginning to stir somewhere deep inside. What is it that's missing from your life? What would make it more complete?

▶ PAGE 16

4. Now write out your list of values in order of importance. If you find your-self stuck between two choices in terms of priority, consider which one you would choose if you could keep only one on your list.

5. Imagine someone you admire who is already enjoying the successful life that you aspire to – someone who, when you look at what they do, makes you feel energized, inspired, alive; someone whose life you would love to be living. Draw up a list of values that must have been important for them in order to get to where they are now. Again, put these in order of priority.

6. What needs to change for you? How do you want YOUR list of values to look in the future? When could you start to bring the changes that you want into your life?

Keywords for ideas

- financial independence • abundance • great body • adventure
- teamwork • career/business • individuality • freedom • boldness
- leadership • creativity • relationships • sport • artistic achievement
- writing • personal style • ambition • work/life balance • travel
- exhilaration • studies/research • spirituality • focus

World-class players work with excellence as their baseline. That is who they are. That is what they stand for and what matters to them. As you 'get the feel' for the level of results they create, the prospect of living a similar life is likely to become increasingly beguiling.

Making change happen

Let other people's success be an inspiration that ignites your own passion. Look at how they love what they do. Experience in your imagination the feelings they must be feeling. The French military writer Ferdinand Foch observed, 'The most powerful weapon on earth is the human soul on fire.'

It's passion that will drive you to achieve; passion that will unearth within you the resources to do whatever it takes; passion that will keep you focused when lesser mortals flag and fall by the wayside. Emotion is a phenomenal driver. Imagine how euphoric you will feel when you hit a goal you had perhaps not even thought was possible. When you can engage with the powerful emotions that will go with your success, that's when you will find within yourself the burning need to bring about change in your life. Once your emotions are searingly hot, it's at that point that your desire for change will become irresistible.

When you have decided on the changes you are going to make, actually making them is quite easy. You just start! Do one small thing that will take you in the direction in which you want to go, something that is manageable and will not be too challenging. Then do it again. Keep on doing it consistently. Add another thing, and keep on doing it. Then another ... If you add one small new step every day for a period of three months, you will have taken almost 100 clear-cut steps to where you want to be. You will find very quickly that the steps don't work in isolation, though. They will soon begin to work with each other and accelerate your momentum. You will find yourself dropping habits that no longer serve you because you develop a clearer perspective on where you need to be. Because you are taking focused, accelerating action in the direction in which you want to go, the quality of your life cannot help but improve! What's more, you will experience how success breeds success. The more successful you become with your small steps, the more energized and excited you will feel about tackling bigger opportunities.

The key is to maintain the discipline of doing what you need to do every single day – no excuses, no explanations, no justifications. Excuses are for losers! Either you do it, or you don't: it's a simple measure. Elite performers deliver on their intentions.

Turbo-powered goals

Goals are great for defining where you want to be and when you want to arrive there. However, people who want to be ahead of the pack look for ways to accelerate that process, to refine it, to obtain greater value for their investment of time, energy and resources. It's about streamlining the process and making it more effective so that results appear faster.

A powerful way to do this is to drop the notion of goals altogether. Goals can be regarded as something we are heading towards in the future, something on the horizon, often just out of reach. Instead, think of your way forward in terms of plans. Plans have a concreteness about them that is directly linked to action. They are inherently based on current reality because making plans implies articulating the steps you are going to take in order to arrive at your objective. They bring about clarity of thinking because you are identifying exactly what you will do, and breaking it down into manageable steps. They imply establishing a timescale for each step – and therefore they also create the opportunity for you to ask whether you really do need to spend the amount of time that you think you do, or whether you could achieve each step more effectively. Could there be a smarter way of doing things? Could you streamline some of the steps? Are there opportunities you could leverage along the way?

Because you build your progress in defined steps, it becomes much easier to measure how you are doing en route. The success coach Tony Robbins alludes to this when he asks, 'How am I going to live today in order to create the tomorrow I'm committed to?' He looks at his objective and examines how effectively each step is taking him towards it.

If you find that you're not sticking to your plans, take the time to ask yourself why. It may be that your objective is not sufficiently compelling – and your life is too short and important to be travelling in a direction that is less than compelling. Or it may be that some details in your plans are not working, and therefore require your attention. Be constantly aware of what is going on for you and adjust your course as necessary.

When I first started working with plans rather than goals, I estimated I improved my effectiveness by about 50 per cent. When you adopt this way of thinking you will begin to find your progress speeding up exponentially because you will be maximizing the value you obtain from each step.

The time for creativity is now

Give yourself permission to fantasize. Children are very good at this; think back to a time when your own imagination knew no limits. Perhaps there was a time when you wanted to be an astronaut, a racing car driver, a nurse, a concert pianist ...? As we become older, we tend to let reality dampen our mental flights.

If your working environment is not all it might be at the moment, for example, let your imagination explore how it would be if you were to escape a life of the mundane. How would it be if you were to jump out of bed every morning and dive into work that you were truly passionate about? How would it be if your life were a succession of 'peak experiences'? What if you were living a life of energized fulfilment, a life where the boundaries between work and play were completely blurred? Visualize a life where work was play and play was work. Imagine you were so in love with what you do that you didn't care if you weren't paid for doing it – but the money just flowed in anyway.

We live in an age of unparalleled creative opportunity, so use it to shape your own life. Use the full potential of your imagination to explore how

EXERCISE **EXPAND YOUR VISION**

Write a few sentences in your journal about each of the questions below. Let your mind roam freely. Ask yourself, 'How could I take this to the next level in my life?' You may like to explore each question on a different day, so as to allow yourself plenty of space to work on one idea at a time. If at any point you feel tempted to shut off an avenue of thinking because you tell yourself that it would be impossible, consider this: 'What would someone who is already a super-achiever be thinking?' Be wild. Be free. Throw off the shackles of the conventional.

- What is the single most wonderful moment of your life that you would love to repeat again and again if you could?

- Can you think of a time when you felt totally fulfilled and absorbed in what you were doing, totally 'in the flow'?

- How are your values expressed in your work? In your personal life?

- What are your best talents and abilities?

- What makes you happy? What inspires you?

- What do you want your legacy to the world to be?

you could bring more fun and magic into your life on a daily basis. Dare to dream!

One of the sad legacies of the industrial revolution that is still with us is the notion that work is 'work' – a grim necessity and often dreary and boring as well. If you subscribe to this view, you are failing to live your life to the full. You are pouring at least a third of it down the drain every day. Your mission as you walk this planet must be to discover how you can serve others to the delight of them and yourself. Anything less and you are short-changing yourself.

You deserve to do work that inspires and delights you. Corporations that understand this and create an inspiring environment in which to work have people queuing up to work for them. Look at Apple, Google, Nike, Southwest Airlines ...

Nike, for example, includes among its maxims, 'It is our nature to innovate'. They see creativity and innovation as core competencies for the organization.

If you have any doubts that a life of fun and rewarding activity might be possible for you, remind yourself that for many people this is their reality. If other people can do it, so can you. If you don't dare to dream about it, you cut off all possibility of achieving it. To echo the strapline that helped build the Nike brand over many years, 'Just do it!'

> *When we are inspired, our energy shifts, we are more aligned with the essence of ourselves. We are in tune with our highest energy, and begin to resonate at a new level. Then we start bringing new situations, events and people into our life that resonate with our new energy. We discover a whole new world ... it was already there, but we hadn't seen it because of our limited perception.*
>
> Nick Williams, *Unconditional Success*

▶ PAGE 24

EXERCISE **CREATIVE VISUALIZATION**

Now try out a powerful technique used by many top athletes to bolster their training. It programmes your subconscious mind with an image of the person you would love to be. You will then find yourself taking actions as if you already were that person.

1. Find a quiet spot where you will be undisturbed for about twenty minutes. Relax, and just let your attention focus on the gentle rhythm of your breathing. As you become more relaxed, let your imagination take you into the future, to a point where your plans have reached fruition and everything is happening exactly as you had intended.

2. Imagine you are watching it all happen on a big cinema screen. The colours are very vivid and intense. As you listen to what is going on around you, the sound seems extraordinarily real. It's as if you were actually there in person. Take a look at who is there with you. What do the clothes that people are wearing look like? Where are you all located? What are people saying? Notice how people are congratu-lating you on your success. Notice, too, how you feel – the exhilaration, the fulfilment, the deep inner sense of satisfaction. Notice what you want to notice.

3. Now turn up the colours on the screen. Turn up the sound. You are so immersed in the action you see that nothing else matters. You become aware of nothing else around you apart from the wonderful experience you are witnessing. It all becomes more and more vivid, more and more real.

4. You become so immersed in the action that it is just one small step from being where you are to stepping right into the middle of the action you

see on the screen – and suddenly you find yourself there, at the centre of all the attention. As you look around, you see your friends and all the people who helped you arrive at this point. Drink in what you see. Hear the details of everything going on around you. Experience the sheer unadulterated excitement of what is going on – take it in to the full.

5. When you feel the action is at its peak, put your left hand on your left knee, squeeze, and hold it for five seconds.

6. Look around your success scene some more. Again, turn up the volume on the experience – what you see, what you hear going on around you, the excitement and sense of achievement that you feel. As you enjoy it all and drink it in, again squeeze your left knee with your left hand.

7. Repeat the process one more time.

8. Finally, still in the middle of your success scene, look back through the screen through which you entered the picture a few minutes earlier. See the present you sitting there, watching it all, and just give yourself a knowing little wink and smile. Looking back from the future you can see it was worth all the effort!

Repeat this exercise daily. It will shape how you think and feel, and therefore what you do. You will also find that each time you squeeze your left knee outside the context of this exercise, all the feelings that you were experiencing will come back to you in an instant. It acts as a trigger, and will immediately put you in the frame of mind of you, the achiever.

Your transformation is underway!

Growing into the new you

Who is this new individual that people will see as you emerge into the next stage of your life? What changes will you and other people notice? How will your feelings about yourself change?

In this first tactic we have done some important work to begin your transformation process. You have identified what is truly important to you and have learned to focus your energy on those areas. You have started to look at how your thinking shapes your actions and at how you can regain control of your thoughts to take you in the direction you intend. You have started to consider your future. You have learned how to use a creative visualization technique to accelerate change within yourself.

Most importantly, you have started to recognize not only who you really are, but WHY you are, why future generations will remember your name. When you live your life to its full potential, you will experience a sense of fulfilment and deep inner satisfaction. The world is waiting for your unique collection of talents, skills and personal attributes, and it falls to you to deliver them – generously, sincerely and with excellence. Only then will your success come into its own. The Hindu writer Patanjali says:

> *When you are inspired by some great purpose, some*
> *extraordinary project, all your thoughts break their bonds,*
> *your mind transcends limitations, your consciousness expands*
> *in every direction, and you find yourself in a new, great and*
> *wonderful world. Dormant forces, faculties and talents come*
> *alive, and you discover yourself to be a greater person by far*
> *than you ever dreamed yourself to be.*

You were born to live an inspired life. Let your thoughts and actions create that life. Be willing to step outside your comfort zone. As your sense of purpose and direction takes hold, you will find yourself achieving more and more.

Let's look, in **Tactic 2**, at what you might do to accelerate your progress.

TACTICS IN ACTION

Rehearsing success in your mind

In my younger years I lived for one of my great passions in life, which was sailing. I loved racing. As I became successful I was often approached by teams who wanted me to train them. One time I was approached by a youth team whose coach was leaving and they needed someone to step into his shoes. I was at first reluctant to agree because I was conscious of their previously formidable success record and I had reservations about my own ability to deliver to the same standard.

In the end I did agree, and when eventually we went out training on the water, my anxiety was compounded, as it was then that I saw that a number of their key members had left at the end of the previous season: the combined skills of the teams were significantly less than I had expected. While there was a lot of enthusiasm, we really had a lot of work to do in order to bring the standard up to competition level, and not too much time in which to do it.

We spent many hours training on the water and in tactical discussions ashore, but all the time I knew we still needed more. It was at this time that I started doing detailed research into how Olympic sailors train. What were the training practices that gave them their competitive edge? How could we harness that knowledge to improve our own performance?

For me it turned out to be the start of a lifelong interest in and passion for the psychology of performance that has brought so much success to my training methods in both the sports and the business arenas over the years.

The first exercise we did as a result of my research into Olympic star performer training was to rehearse mentally the individual actions that needed to be taken during the race in order to secure the competitive edge. Drawn from this concept we worked on the details of where the boats needed to be positioned in relation to each other as they rounded a mark. If the boats were positioned strategically they could find a little bit of extra space to round the mark and also pin down competing boats to let fellow team members through.

I instructed the teams in exactly what was to happen, exactly how to keep the competition pinned down, and what to do to emerge in at least first and second places (which would normally guarantee victory for the team). Together we built up a mental picture of the perfect moves, step by step, and talked each detail through.

▶ PAGE 26

I then told them that all of the team members needed to agree to rerun the drill in their own minds just before they went to sleep at night, and again at the moment they awoke in the morning. The reason for those timings was that the subconscious mind is at its most receptive at those times. Some people were sceptical about it; some even thought it was quite funny. Nevertheless, everyone agreed to do it for a week.

In running and rerunning these mental drills, patterns were being formed in their minds which would automatically trigger actions that would lead to securing winning positions when racing for real on the water. It was as if we had made a video of the perfect race from the winners' point of view and had implanted it in their brains.

When we next went training on the water the results were extraordinary. The transformation was incredible, and the atmosphere among the teams was euphoric.

From that time on, my teams developed a thirst for applying these psychological tactics to enhance their performance. They'd ask, 'Jan, do you have any more of those mind games?' And they then went on to deliver a series of outstanding performances at championship level.

When in later years I started to use similar techniques in business and personal development training, again the results were astonishing and fast-acting. Creative visualization is a powerful performance tool. While it is no replacement for real-life experience, it does have its own advantage in that the perfect scenario can be rehearsed again and again, with the actions becoming engraved on the psyche until they become almost spontaneous in nature.

TACTICS

TACTIC 2
WALK THE WALK

Your schedule is the best barometer for what you truly value and believe to be important.

ROBIN SHARMA

Be who you are meant to be

When you have made the decision that you want to live life with an inspired sense of purpose, that you want to unleash your passion and live life to the full, you will start to experience a number of gear shifts in how you operate. The very nature of your days will change. Your desire to explore your full potential means that you will find it increasingly unacceptable to squander your time, energy and thinking power on things that don't take you along the road you need to travel. You will learn to bypass people and situations that sap your energy and creativity.

You will find yourself noticing things you hadn't noticed before. You will find yourself more receptive to new thoughts and ideas. You will find yourself hungry for the influence of people you see doing what you want to do and enjoying success through it. The American news channel MSNBC once ran an advert that strikes to the very heart of where you are now going:

> *Progress happens when people lean forward.*
> *When we think bigger, listen closer, act faster ...*

This is going to be you. What you find yourself saying will change. What you find yourself doing will change. Most importantly, what you find yourself thinking will change! The power of your decisions, and your commitment to taking focused action in order to create what you want in your life, will start to open new doors – perhaps doors you hadn't even previously imagined. The actions that you take will reinvent your future.

In this tactic we look at the practicalities of making it all happen. What strategies do you need in order to accelerate your progress? What states of mind and habits do you need to develop? What are the personal traits and characteristics that you will need to foster so that you take your rightful place among elite performers? All successful people understand one important fundamental: success is something that you create.

Model successful people

Success is not a mystery. Life works on a cause-and-effect basis. Sadly, most people plod through life blissfully unaware that they are shaping their own destiny. You do one set of things, you get certain results. You do different things, you get different results. As Einstein said, 'Nothing happens until something moves.' You, then, are the architect of the movement that you generate.

Successful people have had thoughts and taken actions that have created their success. If they were to have the same thoughts and take the same actions all over again, in all probability the results they would arrive at would be pretty similar. They designed their own futures and you can design yours, too. It's a matter of selecting the thoughts that will take you where you need to go, acting on them, then sustaining those actions day after day, making small adjustments as necessary along the way.

Learn from people who have already done what you want to do. Why reinvent the wheel? Life is too short for you to discover everything for yourself from scratch. Take people you admire, people who have achieved what you are looking to achieve, and observe them closely. Find out all you can about how they have needed to think and what they did to get to where they are now. All too often people see the glamour and glitz of success, but fail to see the hard work that has gone on in the background. Their success is usually the fruit of a mountain of hard work that is kept hidden behind the scenes. Read biographies, do research online, talk to them ... Successful people, if approached in the right way, are often happy to share their expertise and wisdom. Be willing to invest in the effort to acquire the knowledge that you need, whether it takes the form of sheer sweat, intense focus or, wherever necessary, hard cash. The exercise on pages 32–4 will initiate the process for you as you step into the mindset of serial achievers.

Successful people think in very particular ways. They do not make excuses. Excuses are for wimps. Elite players take personal responsibility for their outcomes. It's not enough to go through the motions. You have to

TACTICS IN ACTION

An epic dream

Lisa Clayton felt she was reasonably successful in life, working first as a chartered accountant and then in the finance department of a holiday company. However, she wondered whether there could be more than this. How to find the excitement and adventure that she was craving? What could make her life feel more whole, more purposeful? She was introduced to sailing yachts by her boss, and soon began to show a natural talent for it. One summer weekend she came upon Naomi James's book, *At One with the Sea*, in which Naomi recounts how she sailed single-handed around the world. Naomi had had problems with the self-steering equipment on her boat and had had to put into port for repairs a couple of times, but nevertheless had circumnavigated the globe – no mean feat.

That day Lisa's life changed for ever. She was inspired. She knew from that moment that she had to sail around the world single-handed, and be the first woman to do so non-stop. She had to surpass Naomi's phenomenal achievement.

Lisa ploughed all her savings into an old, 11.5-m (38-ft) rusting yacht, which she named *The Spirit of Birmingham*. She worked on her day and night to transform her into a vessel capable of taking her through some of the most demanding and treacherous seas in the world. At times she faced unbelievable frustration, finding sponsors and equipping the vessel, while at the same time planning her voyage. There were points when she thought she would never get the project off the ground. Slowly, though, it all began to take shape. She found within herself reserves of passion and determination she had never previously known.

The voyage itself is an extraordinary story. Her yacht was hurled around by angry oceans. She was becalmed for days on end. One time her yacht turned over completely in a storm in the middle of the Southern Ocean, which left her badly shaken but, fortunately, uninjured. She had the most wonderful and exhilarating experiences of her life, as well as days of anguish, setbacks and near-disasters.

Finally, 285 days after setting off, Lisa sailed triumphantly into Dartmouth having broken the record for being the first woman to circumnavigate the globe single-handed and unassisted. She was welcomed back by the Royal Navy, the BBC, the press and a whole flotilla of yachts.

embrace your desired outcomes with passion – 110 per cent – and move with overwhelming energy, understanding and knowledge through every single step. Excuses will always be there for those who want to seek them out. However, if you allow them to appear in your life, don't expect to be admitted to the ranks of the elite. It's one of the choices you have to make early in your journey.

It can be all too easy to think that other people are more successful because they have had better opportunities, have had more money behind them, are cleverer, better looking ... The list can be endless. What we often don't notice is that successful people are willing to be knocked down more often and harder than others, but are willing to pick themselves back up, dust themselves off, and carry on with renewed vigour and focus, again and again. Be willing to do whatever it takes. Just as for the people you admire, your heroes, your future lies in your hands. Adopt the mindset of a world-class performer.

Become who you really are

Once you know who you need to become and what that means for you, start to live the part. Start to live your life every day as if you have already achieved who you need to be. If you want to become a billionaire, it doesn't mean spending money on a lavish scale and maxing out your credit card. Rather, it means putting money aside regularly, investing it well, monitoring your investments daily, every day improving your understanding of how to create wealth, undertaking training to increase your knowledge and investing skills, reading what billionaires read, thinking how billionaires think. If you want to be a world-class athlete, adopt the daily training and diet regimes by which world-class athletes live. If you want to be an explorer, start planning your expedition, doing the research, making the contacts you need, putting the finances in place. If you want to be an author, create a number of hours in your schedule every day to do your research and write. Do it!

▶ PAGE 35

EXERCISE GET UNDER THEIR SKIN

When you see someone else who has already become a success, doing what you want to do, capitalize on the opportunity and learn from it. They have arrived at this as a result of what they have chosen to do. How far can you tap into their experience and put it to use in your own situation? Can you see yourself having the same thoughts and beliefs? Would you be willing to take the same actions? This exercise helps you step inside what has been going on for them. Take about twenty to thirty minutes to explore some new thought processes.

1. Decide who your hero is and focus on that person. Start making some notes on what you observe about their behaviour and about the person you envisage them to be. What do you notice about their appearance and demeanour? What do you see them do? What is the daily reality of their lifestyle? What do you notice about the language they use? What might they be thinking at various points in the day? What does success mean to them? Take your time and absorb as much detail as possible. Breathe it all in.

2. As you begin to notice more of the details, imagine you have actually become that other person. Look around you and see things as you imagine they might see them. Feel the feelings they might be feeling. Let go and play. Drop your inhibitions. Become your hero – just for the sheer fun of it. Experience the shift from being you to being that other person.

3. After a while, start to bring to mind a project that you are working on and that you want to push to the next level. Be relaxed, almost casual. Start to think around your project as if you were your hero. Put yourself in their shoes. How would they see it? What would they be planning to

do? What aspects would they be excited about? What experiences and skills could they draw on? What sort of language would they be using about their future plans?

4. Still as your hero, imagine yourself at some point in the future. See yourself just on the brink of bringing your project to a conclusion. You have only one tiny thing left to do, and it will all have happened. You will be there. How does it look to you? What is it that you see? Turn up the volume on the colours around you. What do you hear going on around you? What do you feel? Enjoy the sensations.

5. Now, still in the headspace of the other person, your hero, reflect back on the steps that you took to get to where you are right now. This will take a little practice to begin with because you have to let go of your own experiences and imagine what the other person would have done. The easiest way is to think of the step they took immediately before now, then the step they took before that, and so on. Let your imagination roam freely. Imagine you are a world-famous actor, growing into your role as you prepare to shoot a movie. The purpose is to explore what someone you think of as more successful than you might have done in your circumstances. Everything has to begin with an idea. If your hero's ideas might be better than yours, could you borrow them? This is your opportunity to give your thinking an upgrade. Continue thinking backwards, step by step, until you reach the point at which you actually find yourself now.

6. Enjoy the experience of letting your imagination run wild. Then, when you have finished the exercise, make notes about any thoughts and ideas that particularly caught your attention. By thinking from within the virtual headspace of your hero, you have taken the opportunity to look at your project from a completely different angle. Success leaves

clues – use them! Become open to thinking differently. Become open to the idea of doing things the way people who are more successful than you do them.

The psychotherapist L. Michael Hall, in his book *The Sourcebook of Magic*, points out:

> *If you know what you want to do and see that it is a human*
> *possibility because others can and are doing it, then there's*
> *a strategy to that experience.*

By getting inside the mind of the person already doing what you want to do, you put yourself in the best position to access that strategy and to expand your thinking. Many people are too timid to do this exercise for fear of what they might find – and that's why they will fail to stand out from the crowd. You, on the other hand, belong among the elite ...

How to get to who you are

Take bold action. Take such momentous action that no one (especially you) can be in any doubt about who you are, about where you are going – and why! Let your spirit come alive and become who you need to be. Be ready to innovate, to excel, to commit to the future you.

In doing so, you will create a formidable energy within yourself. The physical actions that you take will stream messages to your subconscious about the sort of person you are becoming, and will imprint themselves on your inner being. Your subconscious mind, unlike your conscious mind, doesn't test the detailed accuracy of the messages it receives. It just accepts them, stores them and alerts you to opportunities that match the messages it has stored. This is why, as you work with the exercises, you will start to notice things you hadn't noticed previously, and to act on them.

A circle of events starts to evolve. You do what you need to do. The physical process of doing imprints itself on your subconscious. Your subconscious accepts the information as part of who you are and stokes up your desire for more of the same. You do some more. Your subconscious gets the message ... You will find that gradually the edges between acting 'as if' and your perceived reality begin to blur. The gap between the two will start to shrink. There will eventually come a time when you won't even notice the difference between one and the other. You will be on the journey to the new you.

If not now, when?

There are people who put off making decisions and taking action again and again while they busy themselves with minutiae. There are indeed people who virtually take procrastination to the level of an art form. We are all guilty of this to some degree. Each one of us has at some point postponed doing something to which we knew we should be attending. There are many reasons for this. It may be down to a lack of urgency, or not being in the right

▶ PAGE 38

EXERCISE **MAKING GREAT DECISIONS**

Elite players know that making confident, well-considered decisions is an important tool of their progress. There is no room for procrastination or dithering. The quality of their decisions will determine the quality of their results.

Sometimes, there is no easy way to know whether a decision is going to be the right one. However, you can use a structured process to help you. Use this step-by-step guide below to help you work on a decision that you are about to make. Be short and snappy in your answers and write them down in your journal.

Remember, the process of forming the words by hand imprints your thinking on your subconscious, where thoughts and ideas can start making connections of their own accord.

1. What is the outcome you want to achieve by making this decision? Where will this decision take you? Be precise. How will you eventually know that you have made the right decision? What are the feelings you want to experience as a result of the decision you make?

2. What are the options open to you? List as many as you can. If some of them sound a little crazy, that's okay – remember, this is work in progress. The more thoughts you have, the better, and always remember that something that might initially sound a little far-fetched can trigger a thought that is just right, a thought you might not have previously considered.

3. If other people are going to be affected by your decision, ask them what they would do. The more they feel involved in the process, the more likely they are to be receptive to the outcome. Other people may also have a point of view you hadn't thought of.

4. What would be the impact, consequences and any risks for each of the options you might consider? Write them all down in separate columns. If any of the risks are too great, delete that option.

5. If there are any options that would give rise to a conflict with your values, delete them from your list.

6. As you look at the facts assembled before you, you will start to develop a 'gut feel' for the right way to go. Also think around what the impact would be when you achieve your preferred outcome? Do you need any further information or clarification before you can either commit to that option or discard it?

7. Cross-check:
    a. What assumptions are you making?
    b. Is it going to be workable?
    c. If you were to start living with this decision right now, would you want it?

mood; it may be that what needs to be done isn't as exciting as some of the other things on offer right now; it may be that we hope somebody else will take care of it … As human beings we can be remarkably creative in finding excuses for not doing things.

One of the characteristics of elite performers is that they have learned to use time well. Each of us has 168 hours at our disposal each week. While a certain number of those hours need to be allocated to sleeping, eating and dealing with the other basics of life, the remaining hours we can do with as we please. Successful people invariably use their time more effectively than those who are less successful. This stems from three crucial understandings that they have reached:

- The time allocated to being productive (some people call it 'work') is time to be utilized to maximize returns. They expend their efforts on matters that are genuinely important, as far as possible matters that need attention from them specifically. Everything else, they delegate, farm out or consciously drop from their agenda altogether. They reserve their time for high-value activities.

- Each of us needs time to switch off, recharge our batteries, recuperate and just play. This is important, indeed essential, if we are to be creative, dynamically thinking performers for the rest of the time. Therefore, elite performers programme this element into their week and make sure it is observed at strategic points. They take responsibility for their fun.

- They make conscious decisions about how they use time and treat it as their most valuable resource.

If you are not yet taking control of your time, don't expect to be able to change all at once. Instead, take small, progressive steps. Once you have started taking action on your clear decision, you will find that your progress will accelerate. You will begin to find life more rewarding, you will feel more in control, you will be more energized and you will discover more quality time at your disposal.

Use these tips as valuable stepping stones to help you keep your time under control.

- Decide on your highest priorities and objectives, and make sure you direct your energies towards them.
- Plan your schedule for each day – and stick to it! You can download a weekly planning template at www.tactics4talent.com, in the members' area. Make sure you leave some slack for the unforeseen.
- Lay down boundaries for interruptions. Minimize them as far as possible, but make sure you are still openly available to people. Balance is key.
- Delay opening emails until later in the day. That way your attention isn't diverted from your planned agenda.
- If you find yourself putting something off, ask yourself what's behind your procrastination, what is holding you back. If the task feels overwhelming, break it down into small, manageable chunks, maybe even into chunks that each require just a few minutes' work. If you fear the potential success it might bring (or possible failure), enlist support from people who can help you.
- Observe the three Ds: do, delegate or dump.
- When you can see that your time management has improved, acknowledge it and reward yourself accordingly. You deserve it! Then keep up the momentum.

Your life is too important to fritter away. Unfortunately, as with money, we often see this only when it's too late. Take control of how you use your time and watch your success grow.

Treat mistakes like gold dust

Elite performers treat mistakes differently from everybody else. They 'reframe' them. They obtain new meaning from them, access their learning potential and see what they can take from them to accelerate their mission.

Here's the smart bit. Elite performers also use other people's mistakes to learn from and to propel their own growth. That's called leverage. By seeing what not to do from other people's experiences, or by identifying better ways to do things, elite performers can put these principles to work and make their own results happen faster, more effectively and on a bigger scale. Think of it in financial terms. The smartest way to invest is by using other people's money. (How else do you think bankers make their bonuses?) If you can make money without having to use any of your own, isn't that an attractive proposition? The same applies to knowledge. Start to become curious. You have already explored the idea of finding out what works for other people and building your own models based on it. Find out what doesn't work – and put that knowledge to good use, too.

Mistakes are nothing more nor less than the results of actions you have taken or, sometimes, not taken. Successful people are generally willing to make more mistakes than those who are less successful because they are more ready to push their boundaries. However, when they do make a mistake, they make sure they learn from it and obtain maximum value from the experience.

There are people who hold back through fear: fear of making mistakes, fear of what other people might say, fear that they might look foolish, fear that they won't know how to pick up the broken pieces ... Think of how many people are terrified of public speaking, for instance. Yet what is it, after all, other than an emotional response to pictures they have built up in their own minds? (We talk in detail about how to conquer fears in **Tactic 3**.) Do your utmost (and then some) to perform at a peak level, but if you do make a mistake, have the humility to recognize that you are human and have the wisdom to learn from it. Making yourself laugh at it is a helpful trick.

Avoid beating yourself up. Consider, make whatever adjustments are necessary, regroup – and carry on! How much will it matter next week, next month, next year, in five years' time? Who will really care? What difference will it make to someone on the other side of the world? What difference will it make in the grand scheme of things? Shrug it off and move on.

Skip Plan B

In this tactic we have established the groundwork for following your passion. You will find yourself coming to realize that the more you clarify your raison d'être, who you are and where you belong, the more you will find a life of mediocrity unacceptable. There is no room for compromise. You are coming to understand that the only way you can feel fulfilled in your mission is by making it happen. There is no other option. You are beginning to recognize the fire in your belly that is telling you you have to take action and make things happen like never before. You are on the journey of your lifetime – and it's all up to you.

As you become increasingly aware of how other people operate, you will begin to see how successful people have big dreams and then take well-defined steps to bring them into reality. Your hunger to take your place among elite performers will grow because you will see, more and more, that by adopting the behaviours and thought processes of people who have already achieved what you want to achieve, you can create your own success. Small successes will lead to bigger successes. And success feels good!

You are ready to thwart any villains or obstacles that might stand in your way. You are ready to drop any fears or doubts that you may have had. You are ready to develop a momentum that is going to be unstoppable. As Aristotle said, 'We are what we repeatedly do. Excellence then, is not an act, but a habit.'

Be willing to commit to taking powerful action on a daily basis. Be the person you need to become.

TACTICS

TACTIC 3
CONFRONT YOUR FEARS

Fear defeats more people than any other one thing in the world.

RALPH WALDO EMERSON

Use your insecurity as a springboard

We all experience fear. None of us is exempt, not even elite performers. What's different for each of us, however, is how we respond when faced with it. Courage is not the absence of fear. Rather, it's acting despite the fear. Indeed, some people even feel energized by it: that's when they step up to the edge and perform at their most amazing!

World-class players know that when they act in the face of fear they are pushing their boundaries; they are handling the currency of growth. They are trading their emotion for higher levels of personal performance, for the opportunity to achieve something exceptional. Richard Branson, in his book *Business Stripped Bare: Adventures of a Global Entrepreneur*, observes:

> *People in business who have succeeded have swallowed their fear and have set out to create something special, something to make a difference to people's lives.*

If you ever feel tempted to succumb to fear, there are two empowering questions to ask yourself:

- What do I stand to gain by allowing fear to play a part?
- What's the cost to me of allowing fear to hold me back?

It's sometimes easier to push through it when you understand its source. The human mind is extremely good at imagining what might go wrong and presenting all sorts of gruesome details to support its argument. It's simply a defence mechanism, intended to protect you. You need to upstage your mind – find lots of *good* reasons why things will probably go *right*. You need to decide who is going to be in control – your mind or you? Thank your mind politely for its concern, and then make the unilateral decision that your life's mission is too important to be held back by fear. You have things to do, places to go, mountains to climb …

Fear is the breakfast of champions

When I was coaching sailing teams in championship racing I introduced one particular exercise that always brought my students to the edge. This happened as part of their training in close boat-against-boat tactics and competitive strategies for attack and defence. I would explain fast-paced techniques for manoeuvring into positions of advantage and holding those positions against aggressive attack. Then, just before we went out on the water, I would drop in a small refinement to the exercise. I announced that, for each of the practice races we were going to do, the helm, the person steering the boat, would be blindfolded and so would have to rely on instructions from the crew about every detail of what to do.

Not surprisingly, for the teams this was a bombshell. We were to be engaging in close-quarter combat, usually in expensive boats, and the skipper would be unable to see! As we set sail for the stretch of water where we would be training, there was a distinct edge to the atmosphere. Everybody was apprehensive, even downright scared.

Of course, in setting up the exercise I had built in vital background features to ensure the safety of the exercise and all concerned, and I was driving a very fast semi-rigid inflatable boat, which meant I could intervene quickly if I saw that something was about to go wrong.

We set sail, the blindfolds went on, the anxiety increased and the first two boats set off against each other. When they had completed the exercise, the next two boats took their turn, and so on. In every case, as each pair of boats completed the exercise, the euphoria was overwhelming. Not only had everybody transcended a level of fear and pushed their personal boundaries, they had also discovered new possibilities in terms of teamwork, communication and competitive focus. It was always a pivotal moment for every team I worked with.

▶ PAGE 47

EXERCISE IT'S A QUESTION OF SIZE

This exercise will help you bring your fears under control and re-establish your authority over them. Read through it a few times so that you absorb what to do. Then find a place where you will not be disturbed for fifteen minutes or so, and think yourself through each of the steps. Deal with one fear or set of thoughts that is holding you back at a time; if you have a number of issues troubling you, address each one on a separate occasion.

Part 1

1. What is the nature of the particular fear that is holding you back? Is it based on real facts or on things that you imagine might happen? What are the consequences of it all going wrong? – A bruised ego? Bruised feelings? A bruised bank account? Bruised ...? Is it recoverable? How likely is it to go wrong?

2. What could be the benefits of storming through your fears and accomplishing something spectacular? How could your life be different if you were able to pluck up a bit more courage? How would it be if you could have courage delivered by the truckload to your front door?

3. What would be the cost to you of not breaking through your fears? How would you be selling yourself short? What regrets would you harbour – for ever?

4. Which is more important to you – your fears or your possibilities? Make your choice: you have a life that needs to be lived.

▶ PAGE 46

Part 2

You may by now have decided that the time has come to draw a line in the sand, to take a stand over your rightful heritage and cut the ties to imagined negative beliefs that are holding you back. You know deep down that if you conquer your fears, new horizons will open up, some of which you may not even be able to see at present. The time has come to dissolve your fear.

1. Think of the fear as a solid, three-dimensional object. It could be a square block, a cuboid, a ball, an abstract shape – whatever works for you. In your mind's eye, place the object in front of you.

2. Decide that you are the sort of person who is unquestionably bigger than your issues. Is the fear half your size? A quarter of your size? Smaller ...? Look at the size of the problem in relation to yourself.

3. As you look at the physical shape of the problem, notice it suddenly starting to shrink. Let it get smaller and smaller; let the colour start to drain out of it, too; let its energy fade. It's as if all the life is just ebbing out of it.

4. Let its size reduce further until it's about a cubic centimetre in size or less. Let its colour fade to a thin shade of bland grey, becoming paler and paler. Watch its energy seep out until there is virtually nothing left.

5. Finally you are in a position either to crush what's left into oblivion or simply to let it disintegrate of its own accord. Feel the energy of possibility, which you allow into the space that was previously occupied by fear – savour it and ACT on it! Feel the energy. Feel the flood of possibility coming into your life. Feel the freedom you have created grow.

The message is this: be willing to push yourself outside your comfort zone. You can do this every week by building something new into your schedule that you don't feel comfortable doing, but which you know will advance you along the road you need to take. Embrace the opportunity to do it – then do it! By choosing to be an elite player you have chosen to stand out from the crowd, to stand for more, for better, for more successful. Ask yourself: if you stepped outside your comfort zone in the direction of your journey once a week, how different would your life be twelve months from now?

If you find yourself procrastinating over taking action, understand that this is an avoidance behaviour, and is often a sign of an underlying fear. It may be that you are concerned about what other people might think. Perhaps you have thoughts such as, 'It's not the sort of thing I do', 'I shouldn't …', 'I probably wouldn't manage to …' There are people who will find any number of excuses for not doing things. In contrast, elite performers don't allow themselves excuses or avoidance behaviours. They look square on at what needs to happen, then make it happen. It is one of the traits that takes them into the ranks of the elite. Remember: elite performers take action despite their discomfort.

The Taoist warrior

Take your imagination for a ride. Imagine that you have the power and strength of a Taoist warrior. Behind you are years of training and experience. Your demeanour of tranquillity, simplicity and openness to life hide great reserves of inner control, flexibility and utter fearlessness that give you the composure which defines your strength. You have a refined awareness of the details going on around you, and you know that, should anything adverse confront you, you have the ability instantly and instinctively to turn that energy back on itself, without hurting you in any way. Fear can enter your life only to the extent that you permit it. If you choose not to allow it past your threshold, it cannot enter. You are the doorkeeper to your life. You are the guardian of your soul. You are a Taoist warrior.

EXERCISE **ASSESS THE FACTS**

It's human nature to make decisions first using our emotions, then to ratify them with logic. It's just how the sequence of events works. Here is the logic bit. This exercise lets you take a bird's-eye view of your particular issue and gives you a balanced perspective on what's going on for you.

Take a sheet of paper or a page in your journal and divide it into four. At the top of each of the four segments, write the title as in the diagram below. Then examine a decision that has been causing you anxiety and fill in as much information as you can in each quadrant about the issue that you are considering. Just let go. Pile it all in. Let all the secrets and desires from the darkest corners of your rampant mind surface here. No one else is going to be looking, so it's okay to be very honest here about your thoughts, feelings – and dreams!

When you have completed this exercise, you will see the true nature of your fear and understand where your opportunities lie, enabling you to break through to a new level of achievement.

What will happen if I do this?	What will happen if I don't do this?
What won't happen if I do this?	**What won't happen if I don't do this?**

The very concept is so far off your radar it doesn't register. So how can you make yourself relate to this? What is it you need to do to get the tactical advantage over any negative energy? As a Taoist warrior you know it's not about using force, but rather harnessing the power of your mind and will to use that energy to disrupt itself.

The key to turning negative energy back on itself is to acknowledge its presence quietly, then simply to carry on regardless. You know it's there somewhere in the background, but you also know that it does not serve your needs right now, and so you choose to keep it at arm's length. Your journey, your plans, your future are all too important to let fear stand in the way. You are too strong for that. As you stride on, armed with your courage and resilience, you will gradually notice the energy behind the fear begin to dissipate. Its power will begin to fall off and weaken.

As your confidence increases, so a feeling of exhilaration and empowerment will start to take the place where fear was lurking not long before. Your previous feelings will be replaced with sensations of triumph, conquest – and joy. The experience of crushing a fear in order to take you to your next level of achievement is unparalleled. All it needs is for you to look it squarely in the face, and make the unilateral decision that you are bigger than any fear that might dare to cross your path. A whole lot bigger!

Take action

How do you actually implement your newly emerging courage into your actions? How do you make the transition into the person who strides boldly where they need to go? You will find the answers in your mind, ready to be acted on just as soon as you give your consent. The moment you have agreed to yourself that it's okay to move onto a new level of thinking about your fears, the moment you have embraced change and the incredible power of your mind, is the moment that your transformation begins.

You may have been hurt in a previous relationship and be afraid of being hurt again. You may be scared to ask your boss for a raise or better working conditions. You may be frightened of embarking upon a new career or taking up a project you have been toying with for some time. You may be wary of the prospect of success, or simply of the unknown. Whatever it is that you need to deal with, decide now that you are going to act as if you are the person who has already conquered the fear and have become the new person you need to be. It may feel a little uncomfortable to begin with, but your system will get used to it and the time will soon come when it no longer feels uncomfortable.

Just start living the part. Take small steps at first to build up your confidence. Do something relatively insignificant, something of which you might previously have been fearful. It may be having a conversation you have been dreading. It may be tackling the diving board at your swimming pool. It may be trying a new sport. Let yourself grow into the part of the new you, rather like a character actor. Stand like a person who has done it. Walk with the swagger of a person who has done it. Talk with the confident language of a person who has done it. Do it!

The author and success coach Jack Canfield says in his book *The Success Principles: How to Get from Where You Are to Where You Want to Be*:

> *Successful people exude self-confidence, ask for what they want, and say what they don't want. They think anything is possible, take risks, and celebrate their successes.*

Be bold. Start to enjoy the experience. The physical process of taking action sends messages to your unconscious mind about who you are and the person you are becoming.

Lose the need to have to control everything. Sometimes people fear that they might make the wrong decision. Remember that rarely can anyone know 100 per cent that they are making the right decision when they make it. Assess the facts, make a considered judgment, then act. Look for the possible. Set out to make a difference.

TACTICS IN ACTION

My turning point

My hope for our work together is that as we examine what eminent and successful people think and do that underpins their achievements, you too will quickly start to use the same strategies to create a more rewarding future. However, at this point I'd like to share with you a pivotal moment that transformed my own experience of fear.

I was working as a professional musician at the time, in my early twenties and very early in my career, and had been booked to do a concert as pianist for the great Polish bass singer Marian Nowakowski. Marian had a formidable reputation for his performances at the Royal Opera House in London as well as his oratorio and concert performances. To be invited to share a concert platform with such a renowned singer was therefore both an honour and, I felt, something of a challenge.

We were performing in Manchester and Marian had sent me his music, well marked up, beforehand. We met to rehearse in the afternoon of the concert, but in order to preserve his voice Marian wanted to rehearse only the beginnings and endings, and a few passages where I needed to be aware in advance of what he would be doing.

The concert was a sell-out. As we were waiting to go on stage in the evening, Marian sensed I was nervous. (In fact, I was secretly wishing I'd brought a spare pair of trousers, just in case!) He put his hand on my shoulder, told me how thrilled he was with how the rehearsal had gone in the afternoon, and now was the moment to go out, have fun with the audience and just have an amazing time. He said to me, 'Just think of them all as long-lost friends and go and enjoy.' That warm expression of appreciation and confidence in me was transformational.

We went on stage and, as I saw the sea of 'long-lost friends' welcoming us, I felt a surge of empowering adrenaline sweep through me. I knew from that moment that we would have a lot of fun. We did a stonking gig, and, if I remember rightly, two encores.

Marian helped me to reframe how I looked at what we were about to do, enabling me to restructure my attitude in an instant. It transformed not just my performance that night, but was a guiding thought for many years that followed. In future years, whenever I saw that a musician needed a bit of support before a concert, I would remember that moment and was always very happy to pass the favour on.

As you build up your confidence, you will find the very language you use to talk to yourself will change. That's because a different you is emerging. Your unconscious mind starts to find new ways of seeing things. You will find yourself making interesting choices between what you find acceptable and what no longer serves you. Courage is a key characteristic of elite performers. If you belong among the elite (and undoubtedly you do, or you would have stopped reading by now), your actions need to be the actions of the elite. Fear is not going to stop you!

The other side of the coin

While not everyone relishes fear, for some the adrenaline rush it brings propels them to surpass themselves. It's about finding ways for the mind to take control and push personal limits, making them feel alive. As Mark Twain said, 'Courage is resistance to fear, mastery of fear – not absence of fear.'

The Norwegian extreme artist Eskil Rønningsbakken performs balancing acts as works of art. He has been known to ride a bicycle upside down on a wire 1,000 m (3,280 ft) above a Norwegian fjord. He has balanced on an ice cube measuring 60 by 35 cm (23 by 14 in) that itself balanced on two ropes stretched between two cliffs high above a waterfall. He has performed handstands on a chair, which itself was balanced on a pole, high up on a rock wedged between two cliff faces. He says, 'What I do is draw a picture with vulnerable human beings and their bodies, in the surrounding of mother earth. That's the balance between life and death, and that is where life is.' It's difficult not to be inspired by such a beautiful vision.

Even Rønningsbakken is not exempt from fear, though. He has said:

I feel fear, of course I do, we are humans and we have a natural sense of self-preservation. However, I must control that before I undertake any new project because that would lead to lethal mistakes. If I ever find myself totally fearless, that is when I will stop what I am doing.

▶ PAGE 55

Other, perhaps slightly less extreme activities, such as circumnavigating the globe single-handed in a yacht, walking across the Arctic Circle or even bull-running in Pamplona, may still not be to everyone's taste. However, for those with an appetite for living on the edge, fear is part of the motivation behind what they do. It's about living in the space of personal challenge and making exceptional conquests. People who enjoy living on the edge often say that once they are inside the activity they transcend the fear and are 'in the flow' or 'in the zone'. They are completely absorbed in concentration and adrenaline, followed by an overwhelming sense of exhilaration and personal triumph. It's what makes their blood run hot.

Your time has come

Once you have taken command of the demons of your fears and insecurities (and yes, we all have them!), you will be ready to play the leading role that you were born for on the world's stage. We have devoted much of this tactic to practical exercises because fear is often such a big factor in hindering our performance. As human beings we seem to have a natural tendency to let fear into our lives too easily. Either we allow it to stop us from doing what we might otherwise do or we do things from a state of fear and so don't perform as well as we should. Either way we fall far short of our true potential.

Come back to these exercises often, because by using them regularly they will help you grow in strength and will be instrumental in helping you create the changes that you are looking for. Taking control of your fears allows you to reshape your attitudes, to redefine who you are and to take your performance to a whole new level. You will also find the nature of your interactions with other people changes. As you operate from a position of inner strength and composure, people will become increasingly aware of your leadership qualities and will look to you as a source of strength.

In **Tactic 4** we move on to examine what you need to do in order to facilitate your emergence from the crowd and to establish your credentials as an inspirational leader.

TACTIC 4
UNDERSTAND POWER

A life isn't significant except for its impact on other lives.

JACKIE ROBINSON

Stand out from the crowd

Today people are clamouring for strong, inspirational leadership like never before. Many people feel that there must be more possibility to their lives and their achievements, more opportunity, more to be had if they could discover the way (or had someone to take them there). It follows, therefore, that there are unprecedented opportunities for elite performers to shine and take their place at the front. Of course, the competition is becoming more intense because more people now want to emerge from the crowd, but that's good because it pushes you to reach out further than you might otherwise do, and to excel. I remember a friend once saying to me, 'There is always room at the top, though standing room only.'

The process of selecting the natural leaders in a group is not unlike that of shopping, although it usually happens at an unconscious level of thinking. Studies by behavioural psychologists have shown that, when shopping, people are generally in pursuit of the feelings that ownership of something will bring rather than the actual fact of ownership itself. Management guru Peter Drucker says:

> What the customer buys and considers value is never a product. It is always a utility, that is, what a service or product does for him.

By having what they want, people want to feel more fulfilled, happier, better looking, whatever it is that they are looking for. So it is, too, for people identifying leaders, whether that is in the workplace, an organization they belong to, or a social, personal or sporting environment. People are hungry to be inspired by someone whom they believe will take them to new levels of possibility. They want to experience the energy and propulsion that will enhance their life's journey. They want to associate with individuals who will open up new horizons for them.

Step to the front

Companies and organizations look to bring on board leaders who will help them be, do and achieve more. Individuals are looking for people and circumstances to help them be happier and more successful. Most people don't have the clarity of thinking to be able to articulate exactly what it is that they want. However, when they do see it, they invariably feel drawn to it. It may be that they don't have the time to think too much about what they want for themselves. It may be they don't see opportunities that they could create for themselves.

Therefore, when you step up and start to deliver on possibility, people will notice it, usually first at an unconscious level. When they feel intuitively that things can happen that resonate with their own hopes, values and aspirations, interesting processes start to appear. People begin to act differently. Their thoughts start to travel along different sets of tramlines. There is a shift in attitude. This is the basis of effective leadership. There is a subtle process that goes on beneath the overt behaviours.

When a new group forms, psychologists observe a number of common behaviour patterns from which the group's preliminary leaders seem to emerge. The people who turn out to be the initial leaders tend to be more vocal than the rest. They make more suggestions, and are the first to make them (even though the actual quality of the suggestions is usually no better, and sometimes less good than those put forward by other members of the group). They are self-confident and give the impression of intelligence. They are seen as strong, and are the first to take action, while followers are content to watch on the sidelines. It seems to be a self-selecting process.

Or is it? Certainly you need to be seen to be playing full out at the heart of the game in order to be a contender. However, as the group dynamic takes form, authorities are challenged. The most vocal people are not often the ones with the most substance. Yet it's substance that will win through, as the group needs to feel that whoever is leading is going to deliver. It's against this need that elite performers then emerge. Because of who they have become over time, a neatness of execution and excellence of delivery reflect a finesse in their thinking. New spheres of influence develop. Elite performers step to the front.

Joined-up thinking

In order to take your place among the elite you may have to do things you have never done before. More importantly, you may have to think things you have never thought before. The people who wield influence and power are invariably those who have the ability to bring ideas together and take them in a new direction to good effect. You don't need the job title of a leader to establish yourself as a leader: you just need to think, do and be as one. You are going to have to think yourself into new, as-yet-uncharted territory.

When I am looking at a tricky business situation I am working on, I often think to myself, 'Somebody will look at this and think of something new and interesting. Who is it going to be?' Of course, as a consequence, I make sure it is me doing the creative thinking, and my purpose in that thinking is to open new doors of possibility for people.

Research by Roger L. Martin, Dean of the Rotman School of Management at the University of Toronto, has revealed an interesting characteristic of successful leaders. He interviewed at length over fifty leaders of high-profile organizations and, in his book *The Opposable Mind,* observes that most of them share a somewhat unusual trait:

> *They have the predisposition and the capacity to hold in their heads two opposing ideas at once. And then, without panicking or simply settling for one alternative or the other, they're able to creatively resolve the tension between those two ideas by generating a new one that contains elements of the others but is superior to both.*

EXERCISE **EXPAND YOUR THINKING**

Take a challenge you want to work on and use these questions to uncover new combinations of thoughts that might help you to find a more enterprising solution.

1. What is the problem here? What is not working?
2. What evidence do I have that the situation is not working or could be better?
3. What factors are preventing a more desirable outcome?
4. What are the possible causes of these factors?
5. What's missing here?
6. What could be possible solutions?
7. Which possible solution could be the most effective and beneficial option?
8. What possibilities have I previously not thought of?
9. If someone brighter and cleverer than me was thinking about this, what would they be thinking?
10. What are the individual steps that could be taken towards the preferred solution?
11. What is the action that needs to be taken now? By whom?
12. What will it take to bring others to my way of thinking?

Be willing to take your time over each question. Let your mind roam the full breadth of your knowledge, experience and wisdom and challenge yourself to come up with insightful answers.

The skill lies in accessing the ambiguity inherent in a particular circumstance and seeing how else it could be looked at and what new options could arise. What new links could be made? What assumptions am I making about the relative importance of the respective elements? Suppose someone from a different cultural background were looking at it. What assumptions am I making about what might be possible? And are those assumptions the best ones?

However, few successful leaders jump into a search for potential solutions to a problem as a first course of action. Rather, it is often effective to look first at the nature of the problem itself. What evidence is there that what we believe to be the problem actually is the real problem? What facts might suggest we are not seeing the whole picture? What if we were to start our analysis from a different standpoint?

If you want to belong among the elite, you need to be willing to make bold, new connections between thoughts, connections that will take you along fresh paths. You need to shape and reshape the patterns of your thinking in order for new possibilities to evolve.

Collaborative endeavour

The nature of leadership in organizations has changed in recent years. What's more, not only is it going to continue to change, but the pace at which it does change is going to accelerate. There are a number of reasons for this.

Great leadership impacts directly on the overall success of an organization. In the case of public companies, this was traditionally measured in shareholder earnings; in private companies the values are often more diverse, with achievement measured as much in social or cultural impact as in financial terms. Organizations that understand the power of inspirational leadership are demanding more from their leaders, and are willing to bring in new policies and working practices, transparency of management and a fostering of genuine trust and loyalty. Leaders who understand the power of inspirational leadership refine and use skillsets that help them build engagement, trust and personal commitment in the people they work with. They are aware that they operate in a competitive marketplace and, through first-class delivery, ensure their skills are always in high demand. They achieve their results through building strong interpersonal relationships at all levels of the organization and by establishing common goals that people feel they can relate to.

Kenexa Research Institute, a talent management organization, conducted research into the relationship between high-quality leadership and shareholder earnings (*Exploring Leadership and Managerial Effectiveness*, 2010). Analysing the results from 143 multinationals, they examined whether there was any correlation between employees' views of their leaders' effectiveness and shareholder earnings. Employees were asked to rate their leaders on five factors:

* Do they have the ability to convey a clear vision?
* How well are they able to handle business challenges?
* Are they committed to high-quality products?
* Do they value employees?
* Do they have the confidence of employees?

Companies that scored in the top 25 per cent had overall earnings per share 5.8 times higher than those in the bottom 25 per cent. When analysed over a three-year period, companies in the top 25 per cent had a total shareholder return SEVEN TIMES that of those in the bottom quarter! The employees in the top 25 per cent also enjoyed a significantly more rewarding working environment than those in the bottom 25 per cent and, of course, this was impacting on their productivity. It's little wonder that effective leaders are in demand.

Successful leaders know that the methods of direction from the top and micro-control that were widespread in times past are no longer relevant today. They understand the need to build strong collaborative relationships, where people are heard, where they believe their contribution matters and where they can find personal fulfilment in the contribution that they make.

Allan Leighton, author of *On Leadership – Practical Wisdom from the People Who Know*, points out, 'Attracting and keeping the best brains is not just a question of paying well, it is about having a stimulating and rewarding working environment.' Bright young minds are no longer the 'corporate lifers' that were once the backbone of many an organization. Many want to contribute dynamically, think expansively and be part of an energized vision that is going places. The best will take their talent wherever they feel it is welcome.

Now score yourself

You can use this information to accelerate your progress and shift your personal performance up a gear. Look carefully at what you need to do to build collaborative relationships and deeper personal engagement from those around you, and formulate plans to put it into action. Work out all the details, the steps you need to take and how you will take them. Devise a timescale. Once a month, take the five values measured by Kenexa (see opposite) and give yourself a score out of ten for each one, to judge how you are performing. In order to score ten your performance really does have to be at a world-class level. For each score, ask yourself what evidence you would need to see in your performance to be able to score yourself one point higher.

Many organizations use words such as 'transform', 'inspire', 'empower', 'enrich' … but do they have more than a superficial understanding of how that might work within their context or of what actually needs to happen? When you show up in your daily activity as someone who delivers at an exceptional level, when you show that these words have a powerful meaning when you use them, your life will change!

Inspire commitment

When you are passionate and committed to what you do, when you are living your life on purpose, people notice – and passion is infectious. As the author of *The Leader Who Had No Title*, Robin Sharma, says, 'A day without feeling inspired is a day that you haven't fully lived.' Know why it is that you are doing what you are doing and make sure you can be excited about it. If not, you are doing the wrong thing. By working through this series of practical tactics, you have already started to reshape your future. If you haven't already done so, put plans in place right now to get the wheels of change in motion.

When you have a deep personal commitment to why you are doing what you do, when you fully grasp why it's important in the grand scheme of things, people around you will begin to share your inspiration. As human beings, we all need to feel that we are a part of something bigger than ourselves. We need to feel that we make a difference in the world. We need to feel that what we do is important and has intrinsic value in its own right, that by doing what we do we add value to other people's lives: the baker who bakes delicious bread for people to enjoy, the optician who helps people see more effectively, the salesperson who helps people make better-informed choices, the computer programmer who makes it possible for people to carry out functions more effectively … The list is endless.

It falls to you as an elite performer to inspire and cultivate passion and zest for life in the people around you, and to help them to grow into their full potential. What is it that they need to hear from you or see in you that will help them feel more alive, more inspired, more capable of achieving? All too often people fail to deliver to their full potential simply because they haven't seen how their contribution could fit into the bigger picture, how their role will make a difference. Often people only need the door to be opened for them a little in order for them to see what might be possible. We are creative beings by nature, and when an idea captures someone's imagination, when they spot a commonality of values that engages their trust and vision, great partnerships and alliances can be formed.

TACTICS IN ACTION

The man who sells dreams

When a talented visionary catches people's interest and inspires in them the feeling that they are part of something exciting and far-reaching, he (or she) creates an influential environment in which people feel they have to be 'in on the action'. Steve Jobs, CEO of the Apple Corporation, is a master at connecting people with the wonder of his dreams.

On the morning of 27 January 2008, some 3,000 people poured into the Moscone Center in San Francisco. Signs saying 'There's something in the Air' adorned the walls. It was the Macworld conference, and it was the morning that Steve Jobs unveiled their latest wonder to the world, 'The MacBook Air, so thin it even fits inside one of those envelopes you see floating around the office.' With that, he walked across the stage, picked up an office envelope that was lying there and pulled out his latest computer. The audience was enraptured.

Jobs wasn't selling products. He was selling dreams. It was a carefully crafted presentation that revealed itself like a movie. Jobs isn't content just to show his wares. He lets the story unfold. He creates curiosity and anticipation. He brings people to the edge of their seat ... And when he does finally reveal his offering, it's like a conjuror who whips off the cloth to reveal what has mysteriously appeared from nowhere. When he declares, 'We're putting a dent in the universe,' he has everybody with him, cheering him on. He creates magic.

Jobs understands the need to obtain emotional buy-in from his followers, and he gives them good reason to do so. He knows it's not enough to have the dream yourself. What's more important is to enable the people around you to have a share in your dream, a look into what might be achievable for them, too, a feeling of possibility and expansiveness of vision.

Of course, Jobs's style is unique and anyone trying to replicate it risks falling flat on their face. However, what can be replicated is the understanding that when you capture people's imaginations, they will follow you – because they want to, because it has real meaning for them, and because it pushes buttons that they need to have pushed.

Have fun

When talented leaders emerge, they do so because other people are inspired by what they see, by their presence, their sense of vision and purpose. However, there is an aspect that can often be hidden from view: that the best leaders know how to perform at a peak level, but they also know how to retreat, recharge their batteries and have fun simply for its own sake. It's only by living a life that is fun as well as purposeful that you can be an effective leader and survive without burning out. Fun, of course, means something different to each one of us, but at its essence lie recreation, enjoyment and refreshment of mind and body. What's important is to create space for personal renewal. It's by striking the right balance every day that we maintain our capacity to live at an optimum level. As human beings we are not built to function as machines. Remember that life is here to be enjoyed. Every day that passes by without you having significant fun is a day that you have let slip by without living it to the full. Yes, it's important to go full out towards your objectives, to give it all you have, but it's equally important to do so within a personal framework, and to take time out to regenerate and renew.

People who enjoy daily life, both at work and at play, also generally feel comfortable within themselves. As a result, they exude a well-founded inner confidence and self-sufficiency that help attract what they are looking for into their lives more easily. It's as if their life is a beacon of light that draws to itself all that is good. Make it part of your life's agenda that you work hard and play even harder.

Enjoy life

Here are a number of things you may like to consider as a starting point on your road to having fun. See also how many of these you can bring about for those working with you:

- Make it part of your core requirements to do something enjoyable and uplifting every day, something that makes you feel happy and fulfilled.

- Inject humour into how you see things and lighten up; self-deprecating humour is great.
- Be adventurous in your thinking: risk a little.
- Do spontaneous acts with colleagues or associates that you wouldn't normally do, just for the fun of it.
- Programme times into your schedule to do physical activities every week – work out at the gym, go for a swim, a run or a cycle ride, have a massage, do yoga …
- Once a week, eat something you have never eaten before.
- Explore new books, movies, music, performance arts.
- Travel; go to places you would not have previously considered.
- Spend quality time with friends and strengthen relationships.
- Develop a zest for life, a zest built on passion, curiosity and pushing boundaries.
- Meditate.

How do you know?

The author Malcolm Gladwell has devoted his book *Blink: The Power of Thinking Without Thinking* to exploring how an instantaneous impression can give a more accurate and complete picture than we might care to admit. He doesn't advocate, of course, that this should form the sole basis of any judgment we make, but rather that each of us gives away to the world more information about ourselves than we think we do. He describes experimental work conducted by psychologist Nalini Ambady in which she showed students three ten-second clips of a teacher in action, but without the sound. Ambady found that the students had no difficulty in assessing the teacher's effectiveness accurately. She then cut the clips down to five seconds and finally to just two seconds, and showed each to other students. She found that, even on two-second impressions, the judgments the students made about the teachers shown were essentially the same as those following a full semester of classes. *Blink* goes on to show how instant impressions play a critical role in forming other people's long-term perceptions.

What is your two-second clip going to say about you? How influential are you? What is the quality of the energy that you project? What is the instantaneous impression you give to the world, before you have even said a word? You have the power to be seen as a leader if you choose to make the decisions leaders make: decisions about who you are, about how you interact with other people, about how you act in the light of a heightened awareness of what is going on around you. And people around you will notice!

Once you have made those decisions, you will start to notice changes happening in your life. They may be small changes at first, but as you find yourself enjoying the success that they bring, you will find yourself wanting more of that success. You will want to know more about what you could do to sharpen up your performance, and to play a bigger role in the story that is your life. Let's now move on to **Tactic 5** and look at how you can become more effective in getting people to join you on your journey.

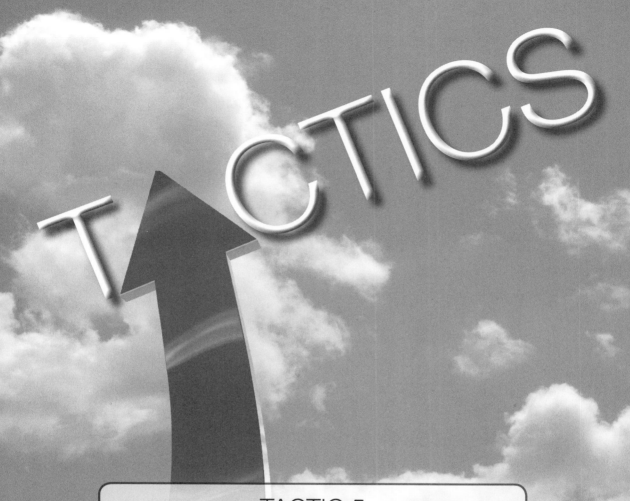

TACTICS

TACTIC 5
PRACTISE PERSUASION

*If you would persuade, you must appeal to
interest rather than intellect.*

BENJAMIN FRANKLIN

Learn to be compelling

Why is it that some people just sound naturally seductive? How is it they can be so effortlessly persuasive? Why is it that, no matter what they say, people seem to feel compelled to follow their every word? It all seems so easy and elegantly straightforward for some people. Although some of us can instinctively get people to respond more easily than others, it is actually a skill that is learned. The fact that the whole process just seems to flow so smoothly simply means that they know what they are doing. They have practised and polished it to get it down to a fine art.

In this tactic we will explore how you can tap into the secrets that will enable you to get people onto your wavelength and influence their actions. We will examine what personal traits you will need to develop in order to boost your powers of persuasion to a world-class level.

You will develop an awareness and understanding of how we can use words and language to influence the world around us. You will see how your choice of words can plant ideas and make people more receptive to your message. You will discover how to affect people's emotional states and reframe how they see things. Great speakers use this understanding to motivate and inspire their listeners to take action.

Step inside their heads

People like to think they make their decisions for themselves, based on their beliefs and how they see the world. If you are going to be highly skilled in the art of persuasion, you will need to master your understanding of this to the point that it forms a rock-solid foundation for your interactions. This is where it all starts.

You will need to see how the world looks through other people's eyes. What is it that makes them tick? What are their preferences? What are their pre-programmed responses? What will they need to see and hear in order for them to respond in the way that you would like?

The more effectively you understand what is going on for the other person, the better placed you will be to create for them the experience that will motivate them to act the way you want them to. The most common mistake people make is to assume that their own model of the world is relevant for the other person. We all see things differently. Failure to take this on board is like trying to have a conversation with another person while speaking a different language. You need to be able to connect. It's okay, it's not for ever. You aren't going marry them (probably)! You don't even have to agree with their view of the world. However, for the duration of your interaction, you need to create a chemistry that will make agreement possible, a spark that will bring about the response that you are looking for. Elite performers have this down to a fine art, which is why they make it all seem so easy.

For that great connection to happen, you also have to see how the other person sees you. People are persuaded by people they like and trust, people who hold (or at least appear to hold) similar values and beliefs to their own, people who understand them. Start to develop a greater awareness of how you come across to the world. What are people seeing in you?

Set the mood

Persuasion is a process of transformation. You are leading the other person from one state of mind to another. A person's responses to ideas and situations are fundamentally governed by their feelings: their emotional state. Where do they need to be with their feelings in order to agree with you? What needs to be going on for them?

The knack to making it work is to create the mood you want within yourself first, then to lead the other person there. Do you want them to be cooperative? Understanding? Sensuous? Do you want them feeling curious or desiring what you have to offer? Work up the mood that you'd like for yourself first, and place it on temporary hold.

When you are engaging with the other person, you first have to meet them where they are emotionally. If they are subdued and you come across all fired up and raring to go, a connection is pretty unlikely. Instead, mirror the energy they are putting out, establish rapport and then take them to the emotional space you have prepared. Begin by using language similar to theirs. Use a similar tone of voice and speed of speech. Then, gradually take them to the speed of speech you want: for persuasiveness, fairly slow speech and a low vocal pitch are most effective. Make sure, too, that your body language is open and receptive. As your rapport grows, you can start to lead them to your emotional space.

As human beings we instinctively copy the nature of any message. Perhaps you can remember a time when you were talking with someone who had lost their voice? Were you tempted to speak to them in a whisper? If someone approached you and started talking sharply, very soon you would feel tension growing within your body and would feel inclined to respond in a similar manner. You have the power to create the mood you want by how you say things. Once you have established rapport, simply tap into this natural response mechanism to take the other person with you on your journey.

Skilfully prepare

Suppose you want to come across as irresistibly seductive. At risk of stating the obvious, remember that the conversation has to be about them, not about you. First, you must prepare yourself. Think back to a time when you felt really sexy and seductive. Your charms were irresistible, and the feedback you were getting was confirming everything you had hoped for and more! You were enjoying a warm glow. Every moment just felt delicious. How did your voice sound? How were the words coming out? How fast were you speaking? Were there any momentary pauses or lingerings? Relive the moment all over again. Listen to how you sounded. Let the feelings you were experiencing saturate your whole body from the top of your head to the very tips of your fingers and toes. Think back to how good it felt and enjoy the occasion all over again. (If you were never very good at it, pretend that you were, and imagine what it would have felt like!)

In the same way, you can create whatever emotional state you want. Simply put yourself into that state first: feel the feelings. Think the sort of thoughts and feelings you might be experiencing, use a tone of voice to match the moods, choose words that match the mood you want to create. Eventually you will be able to trigger this state within yourself very quickly and easily. It will become part of your toolkit as you learn to plan more of what you actually want to say before you say it.

Do you want someone to feel excited? Perhaps you want them curious? Do you want them to buy into an idea? You can apply this technique for whatever emotional state you want to create in the other person in order to obtain an optimal response. Richard Bandler, one of the founders of NLP (neuro-linguistic programming), based much of his work on establishing the right mood for the person to be receptive to the message. He has a slightly tongue-in-cheek way of explaining it, but it gets straight to the point:

> *My sales training program goes like this: induce wanton buying state, then point to product.*
>
> Richard Bandler and John LaValle, *Persuasion Engineering*

Build rapport

Rapport is when you and another person are connecting with all of your senses, sometimes described as being 'in sync'. It's crucial for great communication to take place, a state where common thoughts and ideas can gel and inspired exchanges take place. It happens at an unconscious level, with both parties perhaps merely somehow feeling comfortable with each other. Generally, we tend to prefer people who most resemble ourselves, whether that is in how they look, what their preferences are, what they do ... We tend to feel comfortable with them, trust them and start to make assumptions that their views of the world will be very similar to our own.

When there's a match in our appearances, we often feel there's a basis for a deeper connection and trust. As science shows that physiology plays such a large part, no less than 55 per cent, in our successful interactions, it's a good place to start. If we match the other person's appearance, we set the scene for a closer level of involvement. We do this in one of two ways, either by matching (where we do exactly what the other person did a few seconds later) or by mirroring (where we create the mirror image of the other person). For example, they might place their left hand over their right hand. A few moments later you might do the same (matching) or you may place your right hand over your left hand (mirroring).

As you do this, it's important not to mimic the person, as that would just look silly or insincere. It needs to be more subtle. Take a few moments before you give this reinforcement – and make sure it looks natural. Cross-matching is an even more discreet alternative. For example, if the other person crosses their legs, you might, after a few moments, cross your arms. It will feel a little artificial and contrived at first, which is why you need to practise it in situations that don't matter. Once learned, it will soon become almost second nature. Of course, what we're doing here is what people who have a rapport with each other do all the time anyway at an unconscious level. Here we are just bringing unconscious behaviours to a state of awareness so that you can practise them.

There are lots of aspects you can match: posture, tone of voice, volume of voice, speed of speech, key words and phrases used, speed of breathing, eye contact, eye blink rate ... When speaking on the telephone you can match the vocal qualities that you hear very easily and effectively. You will also be more attuned to the particular words and phrases the other person uses, and start to use similar expressions yourself. Just go out and have fun with it. You might like to try it with friends, at the supermarket checkout, in a coffee bar, at the bank ... As you become better at this technique, you may like to start giving yourself a score out of five for how well you did. Very soon it will begin to flow easily and naturally.

This is the first stage of building rapport. As it grows you will reach a stage where you will do something and the other person will follow and

EXERCISE **READING THE SIGNS**

As you build rapport you will notice small, subtle physiological changes in the other person that will tell you they have experienced a shift internally. This will make you more aware of the situation and enable you to move ahead accordingly. Such awareness is called sensory acuity. Once you become more proficient in observing the minute signs of change in others' emotional state, your increased awareness will help you respond to the them much more intuitively.

There are five small changes that can occur. These are:

- Skin colour – from lighter to darker.
- Skin tone – from matt (not shiny) to shiny.
- Breathing – from normal to faster or slower.
- Lower lip size – from thin to fuller (notice fewer lines as the lip fills out).
- Eyes – pupils dilate from smaller to larger and become more focused.

Choose one sign to look out for. When you meet someone and are having a conversation, look for the slight change as your rapport grows. Be careful that you actually do see the change and don't just imagine it. With practice, you will soon become proficient. When you do see the change, just notice that you have noticed. You will instinctively start to respond more warmly and openly, and the rapport will grow. You will, of course, be doing only what you would normally do. It's just that you are accelerating the process and creating an environment for great communication.

It's easiest to look first for just one physiological change, but when you are more comfortable, add another change to your repertoire, and so on until you have adopted all five. We are all different, so you will find some changes more pronounced than others in different people.

match what you did. You will then be leading; this is a good indicator of rapport and you will be well placed to take your discussion forward. Be patient in this process and, if the following behaviour fades, just go back to matching and mirroring for a while again. Think of it as building synchronicity with the other person – mentally, physically, emotionally. It's a constantly fluid situation.

As a short-cut to gaining rapid rapport, when you meet someone, simply look at them as if they are a close friend you haven't seen for a long time. Take a split second before you let a warm smile fill your face. Let your eyes light up. By adopting this mode of thinking, your body will naturally fall into place and create an openness of stance and a welcoming manner that the other person will most likely return.

Develop trust

At the very core of all effective persuasion is trust. It is not conjured up out of thin air by successful people, as if by magic. It evolves. It's something you build as a result of what you do and who you are as a person, an individual with strong beliefs, principles and ethics. You can't buy it. You can't borrow it. Only other people can award it to you, based on what you do. What it means in practice is that, as people see your underlying traits and behaviours, they feel able to have confidence in you and rely on your integrity. The message you put out is not just the words, but everything that you do and what you stand for. The message also conveys that you are interested in and care about them.

Check out your performance in each of the following traits. They are the cornerstones on which trust is built.

- **Be known as someone who always keeps their word** People need to know they can count on you, so always do what you say you will do. Cancelling or falling short are not options. Your credibility stands or collapses according to how well they can rely on you.

Paying attention pays off

It was a Wednesday evening in May 2004. Tobias Meyer, worldwide head of contemporary art at Sotheby's in New York and the house's principal auctioneer, was auctioning a painting by Picasso, *Boy with a Pipe*.

There had been quite a stir in the art world, not least from the financial standpoint. People had been asking Tobias whether he thought the Picasso would 'achieve' $70 million, which would make it the most expensive painting ever sold at auction at that time. The world's press had their cameras ready. The bidding was fast and furious up until $60 million. Then it came down to the serious players. Two people were bidding against each other, one of whom was Larry Gagosian, an art dealer. It seemed he was bidding for a client, as he was on his phone the whole time.

Suddenly the action stopped at around $72 million. There were colossal sums of money at stake here. Tobias saw Gagosian go pale. The bid was against him. He closed his phone and was simply looking at the auctioneer. Tobias saw that there had clearly been some sort of shift. With years of experience in reading people and handling delicate situations, he saw that something wasn't quite right. The pressure was on! What Tobias said next would determine the outcome of the sale. The world was watching. The atmosphere was electric.

Tobias knew he had to choose his words carefully. He looked at Larry and asked, 'Sir, do you need more time?'

Larry turned to his neighbour, grabbed his phone, quickly dialled a number and placed the next bid. The battery on his phone had died and he had been unable to talk with his client.

The auctioneer could easily have dropped his gavel at $72 million. Instead, with one well-chosen, well-timed question in response to what he saw, the hammer eventually came down at $104,168,000 (to a different bidder) — a difference of over $32 million, which amounted to a cool $11 million in commission for the auction house.

- **Be truthful** When people know that you are honest, they will know they can trust your word. If you need to say something unpalatable or tricky, rather than hiding behind a white lie or concealing some or all of the truth, see if you can reframe it into something more positive.

- **Be transparent** Volunteer sincere and full information to show you have nothing to hide. Tell people as much as they want to know. Be your full self and avoid omitting important details.

- **Share your secrets** This doesn't mean opening up the whole of your life to the world, but a secret or two that may be shared safely can build the bonds of a relationship. Very often, too, the law of reciprocity kicks in, with the other person sharing as well. Make sure you are known as someone who keeps other people's secrets tightly secure.

- **Display integrity** Be seen as a person with rock-solid moral and ethical beliefs and as someone with the social and interpersonal skills to make those beliefs hold up in your daily life. Be consistent in your behaviour and develop your reputation as someone who has concern for other people's well-being.

- **Show your feelings** Be genuine and open. People need to feel they are relating to a real human being, with emotions, desires and needs.

- **Be competent** Show high-level performance in your professional life and let people see that you have a vision for yourself. Be known as someone who takes their future plans seriously and who will not be derailed by obstacles.

- **Be willing to apologize** We all get it wrong sometimes. When that happens, admit your mistake as soon as possible, take personal responsibility for what happened and apologize sincerely. Make sure the people concerned know what action you will take to prevent the same thing happening again.

Look the part

How you come across is crucial not only to your power to persuade, but indeed to the whole of your success strategy. Consider how people see you – that's who you are for them. People respond most readily to others who seem to reflect their own beliefs and values, and this extends to personal presentation, too.

Imagine you are looking for a new dentist and you have to choose between two. Both are eminently qualified and experienced. One is neatly groomed, wearing a smart dentist's smock and has a 'clean-cut' look about him. The other is somewhat scruffy, and is casually dressed in clothes that have clearly seen better days. Which of the two would be your choice?

Most people would choose the formally presented dentist because they would make an unconscious assumption that he will be better at his job. He would match their expectation of what a dentist should look like. The same applies to you. If you are going to be persuading someone, the implication is that you have the moral authority to do so. How you present yourself is part of the credibility factor that will determine your success or otherwise. How you look is part of the 'message' about what you're trying to say. There are times to look casual; there are times to look smart. Getting it right according to the circumstances is the right thing to do.

Successful people make sure their clothes reflect who they are and the impression they want to create. They have practised a confident smile that makes people feel special. They have a firm (but not vice-like) handshake that goes out straight, not at an angle. If it feels like shaking hands with a herring, it's a pretty safe bet that any future interaction will be of a similar nature. (And yes, this applies to both men and women.)

Your posture needs to be straight, but relaxed. Imagine you have a piece of string coming out of the top of your head and someone is pulling on it from above. Great posture looks attractive and exudes confidence.

Armed with these essentials, you are ready to prepare your approach.

Wear the other person's shoes

The more effectively you can see life from the other person's standpoint, the better you will understand what is going on for them, and the more effective a persuader you will be. It's part of human nature to respond in any situation in a way that the person believes will create the best outcome for them. This is not usually a conscious thought process, but rather an automated one. Therefore, the easier you can make it for the other person to want to act in a particular way, the better your outcome will be. Find out as much as you possibly can about that person's preferences, ways of thinking, beliefs and values – and give them what they need to see and hear on a plate.

In **Tactic 9** we will be looking at how to steer conversations in a particular direction through the language that we use, which will further enhance your powers of persuasion. First let's turn our attention to sharpening up the necessary thinking for hot negotiation strategies.

EXERCISE **NINE-STEP PERSUASION STRATEGY**

Use this step-by-step process to plan your persuasion strategy. You may like to practise it on something unimportant until you have refined your skills. Maybe you'd like to persuade a friend to try eating something they have never eaten before, or perhaps go to see a movie they might normally avoid. You must always have as your objective a win-win situation, where everyone concerned is happy with the result.

Take something you would like another person to do for you and use this nine-step process to map out your plan in your journal.

1. What is the outcome you want? Be very clear and specific.
2. How does the other person see the situation?
3. How are you going to build your rapport with them?
4. On what points could you be in agreement with them as a preliminary to what you want to achieve?
5. How could you raise the idea in a way that is meaningful to them?
6. How do they need to feel in order to be receptive to your proposal?
7. What benefits to them could they see in your proposal?
8. What do they need to see and hear in order to respond as you'd like?
9. What could you say that would make your proposal irresistible to them?

You may have noticed that children can be unbelievably persuasive when they really want something. Most parents will agree that if a child focuses on something they want very much, they will be remarkably ingenious with their arguments. Yet, without realizing it, they are usually only following this nine-step programme to a greater or lesser degree. It's only as we grow older that our imaginations become dulled and we become more reluctant to push for what we want. Let go and play – you may surprise yourself!

TACTICS

TACTIC 6
USE SMART THINKING

*One of the things I learned when I was negotiating was
that until I changed myself, I could not change others.*

NELSON MANDELA

You get what you negotiate

It's said that in life you don't get what you deserve, you get what you negotiate. The reason there's truth behind this statement is that great negotiators have the ability to take stock of certain factors – what is going on around them, their own position, market forces, their own tactics and strategies – then make their moves based on what they see. Often they see bigger opportunities than might at first appear. They bring wider considerations into the discussion and see where they can create extra value for all concerned.

If you are going to be an elite performer, well-honed negotiation skills – and the smart thinking that goes with them – are an important part of your toolkit. It applies in business, in your career, in your relationships – indeed, in almost every aspect of your life. Consider the research of Leigh L. Thompson, professor at the Kellogg School of Management, in *The Mind and Heart of the Negotiator*. She has observed four key shortcomings that are frequently found, even in highly experienced and effective negotiators:

- Leaving money on the table: the scope of discussions has too narrow a focus, which means that additional opportunities and extra value creation that could arise for all concerned by looking at things in a different context are missed.
- Settling for too little: failure to look for alternative solutions that might be mutually acceptable, but instead agreeing to take a smaller 'slice of the cake'.
- Walking away from the table: playing for all or nothing.
- Settling for terms that are worse than the alternatives: a deal is not just about price (or whatever the prize under negotiation) – value can also be increased through better delivery lead times, financing arrangements, and so on.

▶ PAGE 87

EXERCISE NEGOTIATION

I assume that, like most of us, you like to think you can strike a pretty good deal when you need to. Let's see. Test out your negotiation strategies in these ten questions. (Select one answer per question.) The answers are at the end of the Tactic, but don't look until you have tackled the whole quiz.

1. You are about to put your home on the market and have had it valued at £2.5m. Before you have a chance to instruct the estate agent, a buyer comes along who loves your place and offers you £2.6m cash! Do you:
    a. Do the deal before he has a chance to change his mind?
    b. Haggle?
    c. Tell the buyer you are on the point of instructing the estate agent, who will be happy to take care of the details for him?

2. You decide it's time you had a holiday home in the south of France and have found the perfect little house on a cliff top, overlooking the sea. The price is €700,000. You tell the owner you can raise only €675,000 and she agrees to sell. Do you think:
    a. You've landed a bargain?
    b. There's probably something wrong with the house?
    c. What is the seller thinking? I'll try to get her down even more.

3. You have been offered a job to die for. You want it very much. Unfortunately, the company is only willing to offer you a salary significantly below your expectations, which you find disappointing. Do you:
    a. Accept the job on the understanding that your salary expectations will be met within two years?
    b. Indicate what you believe is the going market rate and hold out for the salary you had in mind?
    c. Probe what is behind the low offer?

4. Your company has been doing business with a particular client for years. The client has indicated that they want to take their business to a cheaper supplier when the present contract expires. Do you:

   a. Warn them that by cutting corners things can turn out more expensive in the long run?

   b. Offer to match the cheaper prices?

   c. Say that you will be sorry to lose them, but you understand and trust you will do business together again in the future?

5. You are negotiating a contract with a prospective client for your company's services in a new market. In the discussions, you are reluctant to be the first to name a price, but your prospect doesn't want to reveal their budget. You see that your prospect is an astute negotiator and you are going to have to name your price soon. Do you:

   a. Name the price you had in mind and hope it's acceptable?

   b. Name a slightly higher price than what you would be willing to accept so as to create room for negotiation?

   c. Name as high a price as you can justify and see what happens?

6. You have agreed the details of a contract for your company to supply assembled components. Just as the negotiations are drawing to a close, your client demands a penalty clause for late delivery that would put a very large hole in your profits if it was ever invoked. Do you:

   a. Agree to the demand knowing that you usually deliver on time?

   b. Reject the demand and hope you don't lose the client?

   c. Try to reduce the size of the penalty?

7. You have been negotiating for three months with a client interested in purchasing your company's services. You know they have been talking to two other potential suppliers. Finally, they call you and say they have decided to go with one of your competitors. Do you:

a. Thank them for the opportunity to bid anyway and ask to be called the next time they are in the market for your type of service?

b. Ask them what it would have taken for you to clinch the deal?

c. Offer to match or even beat your competitor's price?

8. You will be representing your department in a meeting at which scarce resources will be allocated. The pressure is on for you to perform, as a number of departments will all be competing for the allocation. Do you:

a. Pull together clear numbers and statistics to show exactly why your department deserves a significant allocation?

b. Casually meet each of the other department heads who will be present, mention how your projects could benefit them and how you and they might work together more effectively?

c. Do what you can to make sure the case for your department is heard as soon as possible, so that you clearly establish your claim?

9. You and your partner have been planning a three-week holiday of a life-time for many months. Your company is now under pressure to deliver on a number of contracts and you know that your boss will not take kindly to you being away for three weeks. Do you:

a. Ask for the full three weeks' leave anyway?

b. Agree with your partner that two weeks is more appropriate?

c. Put the holiday off for a year and take just one week because you are needed at work?

10. Do you feel that negotiating success should generally be measured by:

a. Achieving a win-win situation?

b. Winning as much as possible for yourself?

c. Seeing how much extra value you can build in?

How do you avoid making these mistakes? What do you need to know in order to stake your claim in a highly competitive world? What practical and thinking skills do you need to develop to be able to obtain maximum value?

Everything you want to achieve will need to be achieved with and through other people. Therefore, negotiation doesn't just come into play for big financial deals or interpersonal crises. Negotiation is also part of the small day-to-day transactions that over a period of time build the successful life of the super-achiever. The more skilled you are at it, the more effective your success will be. What's more, it is a skill that can be learned and refined. When the best negotiators are in action, many people won't even notice that negotiation is going on.

Your opening gambits

The secret of great negotiation lies in the planning and preparation. Great negotiators define the boundaries of play systematically, with a military precision and clarity, well before any exchanges take place, then steer the game within those boundaries. Once you know how, it's actually quite easy! Start with three key steps that will serve as a solid foundation for what is to follow:

Step 1: Decide what you would do if the negotiation failed completely and you had to walk away. What would be your Plan B? That way, you know what the alternative is, and can therefore evaluate great, good and passable outcomes against your other options.

Step 2: Decide on the worst outcome that you would be willing to accept. If the best that can be achieved is anything less than this, you will walk away.

Step 3: Figure out what the other party's walk-away point would be. What would they do if the negotiations were unsuccessful? How far could you press before they walk away?

Then, when you have established the range of possible outcomes to work with, your job as a negotiator will be to obtain the maximum value within these boundaries. Step 2 gives you the bottom line, Step 3 the upper tipping point. It's for you to end up as high as possible between these two points. Find out where the value lies for the other party. Remember that people have different sets of values and priorities, which is, indeed, why negotiations take place anyway. Someone might be willing to pay you a sum of money because they can leverage what they receive from you in return. You, on the other hand, may be keen to release the resources you have got tied up in order to do something else.

Ask yourself, 'How much return can the other side make out of a successful outcome? What advantages could they secure? Why do they want it?'

Of course, they are not going to show you their hand! It's up to you to find out what is motivating them, and this is where your ingenuity has to come into play. You need to find out which market forces might be influencing their thinking and think about any value that might not be immediately apparent. Do your research. Be willing to challenge all your assumptions, even the assumption that you are not making any assumptions! This is where world-class negotiators stand out from the rest. They pull together as much knowledge and information as they can find, and use it strategically.

Be bold in your approach! Whether or not you are the first 'to go', be strong, but only to the extent that you can fully justify your position. You need to be able to say (or at least think), 'We make this offer at this level because ...' – and to sound plausible as you do so. It's imperative that you are 100 per cent confident in your approach.

Conventional wisdom has it that whoever names a price or outcome first loses, because it is capped at that point. It may be that the other party would have gone higher or for a bigger outcome if you are selling, or you might have secured a lower price or better conditions if you are buying, but once capped rarely is that cap breached. However, there are times when it is useful to make the opening offer. If, for example, you suspect the buying

TACTICS IN ACTION

The merger

A meeting was taking place in Regensburg, Germany, between a very large and well-known Japanese company and a very large and well-known German company. They were in merger/acquisition negotiations. In many ways the companies were very similar, but each had a very distinct culture.

At the eleventh hour, although the initial agreement had been that the German corporation would have at least 51 per cent no matter what, the Japanese now insisted they had to have at least 51 per cent – and would not budge! The Germans had retained a negotiation specialist, Michele Wilke, to help them clinch the deal, and had done a considerable amount of training with her beforehand. They were prepared. They were ready to draw on their training and simply didn't react.

They kept their cool, slowly and quietly sucked in air between their teeth, slightly rounded their posture, did not make direct eye contact, paused for about fifteen seconds, and then one man simply said, 'We are so sorry. No.' They averted their eyes to keep them just at the chins of their Japanese counterparts, allowing the very long pause to remain exactly where it needed to be: absolutely in silence.

They remembered what they had been taught: never, ever, break the silences (and sit tight, outside your comfort zone if necessary).

The Japanese counterparts waited for a very long time before responding. Almost all at once, they rose and walked out. They flew back without ending the negotiations. The Germans looked at Michele, who had been training them, faces shocked and almost speechless.

Michele, who was as calm as ever, simply said, 'No worries, they'll be back.' She could tell, both because of her instinct based on years of experience and because the Germans did not lose face due to their impressive composure. Also, she knew the Japanese would not have gone to all this effort to walk away. They of course knew that the Germans would get 51 per cent: that was the initial agreement. However, the Japanese were power-playing, and they were very good at it, too.

Three days later, they contacted the Germans, then came back to sign the contract, finish the due diligence, and thus seal the merger/acquisition. The Germans got their 51 per cent after all, as had initially been agreed.

party might make you an outrageously low offer, by making an ambitious first offer it is often possible to influence their values and bring them up to the level of expectation you had previously defined for yourself.

Bite your tongue

When you have made your offer, there remains just one more thing for you to do. Shut up! Give the other side plenty of time to consider your offer. Many people find silence awkward and proceed to fill it with verbiage. It's natural to want to talk and be heard. People often begin to make excuses, give explanations and, before they know it, they've talked themselves out of the deal. Make your offer, and then sit tight. Wait as long as it takes. Develop the personal discipline to be comfortable with silence. Let the other side come back to you in their own good time and then, once again, don't feel rushed to fill the space. Take your time before making your considered response.

If you have pitched your first offer aggressively, recognize that you are going to have to make some concessions. However, the other side needs to see that it causes you pain to make those concessions. Be generous in creating time-space as you deliver your 'performance'. It takes a little practice to judge how to use the space of silence, but it's a technique that, once learned, pays off handsomely. It also helps to create the impression that you are a strong negotiator.

Listen

The authors of *Negotiation Genius*, Deepak Malhotra and Max H. Bazerman, have a great take on raising the stakes:

> *A good negotiator will do whatever it takes to* close *the deal, while a negotiation genius will do whatever it takes to* maximize value *in the deal. A good negotiator plays the game well; a negotiation genius changes the nature of the game itself.*

Raising the game in this way means bringing in additional factors, perhaps previously unconsidered, that might add value. To do this you need to know what's going on for the other side, and the way to find out is by listening and asking questions. Be a proactive listener. Find out what is really going on for them. Remember: aspects that you consider important are not necessarily equally important to them. They have their own agenda.

If the other side is holding out for something, find out what lies behind it. Why do they want it? Could you help them with logistics, or financing, or support ...? What will become possible for them by achieving this concession? Might there be other people or situations involved that we don't know about? It's often the case that, once you understand these crucial factors, you will find yourself able to approach the negotiation with more creative ways to structure the deal. You may even be able to give the other side more of what they want than they are actually asking for, at little or no cost to yourself. You will find yourself uncovering new ways to build in extra value.

Build trust

In order for the other side to open up to you, there has to be an underlying sense of trust: without it you will find it very difficult to make any real headway. Your opposite numbers need to feel that you understand their interests and standpoint, and that you want to help make it work for them. It's about building the relationship and establishing confidence in each other.

Time spent building confidence as early as possible in the negotiation is time well invested. Ask yourself, 'What is it they need to feel and see about me and my side that will enable them to open up?' Make it your business to build a strong, trusting relationship, and then to keep building on it.

Engage them in meaningful conversation outside of the negotiations. Make it possible for them to feel comfortable with you. World-class negotiators reach their level of skill by learning to see things through the eyes of the other side, and to adapt their own stance in response to what they see. Very often, the best breakthroughs happen outside the formal negotiating environment, when people are relaxed and connecting on a personal level. It's not a myth that some of the biggest and best deals are concluded on the golf course. When people interact at a personal level and relate to each other's needs, solutions appear that might not be visible in a formal context.

Negotiate your salary

Many people will encounter some of the most important negotiations of their life when agreeing their salary. Yet, astonishingly, most people consistently lose out because they omit to prepare for these discussions in a structured way. When you do negotiate a great salary package for yourself, it's invariably a deeply satisfying experience. It's also something you owe to yourself to be able to do well because it will determine the standard of living you will enjoy as well as define how your future career will develop. Most importantly, it's corroboration by the marketplace of the value you attach to your services.

According to research conducted for *US News & World Report* (1 November 1999), a 22-year-old who is able to negotiate $2,000 extra in annual salary in their first job will, in all probability, generate an extra $150,000 over a career spanning forty years simply because of the compounding effect during that period. Of course, for someone negotiating a $100,000 job, even a 10 per cent improvement as a result of negotiation is going to bring about a colossal return as their career unfolds.

To prepare for your own negotiations, work through the set of questions that follows well before the time comes to do the actual haggling; this will give you the core structure of your preparation. Once you have the strategy comfortably under your belt, you will be able to use the same format in many negotiating situations – not only in terms of your salary – and you will develop a reputation for your effective negotiating skills, too. As with so many of the other processes in this book, I urge you to write your thoughts down. The physical action causes the ideas to ingrain themselves on your subconscious, where your thinking can evolve and grow.

- What are the current market factors around your position?
- What makes you the candidate of choice?
- What is the lowest salary you would accept?
- What would you do if you didn't achieve the outcome you want?
- What good reasons would your employer have to meet your requirements?
- What is the best offer they are likely to stretch to?
- What is their likely walk-away point?
- If the employer is unable/unwilling to meet your salary expectations, what other factors could be negotiated?

Also think about:
- Increased holidays?
- Job title?
- Fast-track promotion?
- Smarter office?
- Moving allowance?
- More accommodating start date?
- Travel perks?
- Share options?
- Other benefits?

Is there anything else that you could bring to the table to ease the negotiation through? If a significantly more effective negotiator than you were looking at this situation, what would they be thinking?

Always work on the assumption that your salary is negotiable. Never ask. If you enquire politely whether there might be some room for negotiation, you will most likely be given the answer you deserve! If you find it difficult to haggle for yourself, pretend you are doing it on behalf of somebody else. Become your own client, and let your negotiator persona become your agent. There are career coaches who charge a four-figure hourly rate to negotiate salaries for top executives. Be your own coach, working for you: you will surprise yourself at the difference it makes. If you were advising somebody else what to think and say, what would your advice be?

Be open to surprises

There was a time when many people thought of negotiation in terms of how big a 'slice of the pie' they might obtain for themselves. The assumption was that the size of the pie remained fixed, and therefore it was simply a matter of who received what. By implication, the bigger the share you managed to achieve for your side, the more successful your deal had been.

Modern negotiation thinking has discarded this notion. Innovative negotiation establishes an environment where creative thinking plays the lead, where each side tries to understand what the other is trying to achieve and to help them do so, and where both sides work together to see if they can find added value where perhaps it was previously difficult to uncover. Expert negotiators prefer to negotiate with other expert negotiators, because they know that their opposite numbers will understand the nature of the agenda, and will work at an appropriate level: both sides are interested in a high-level outcome all round.

The quality of the relationships you build will have a significant impact on your results. When people bring together the collective energy of mindsets that instinctively side-step conventional ways of doing things, remarkable and innovative results are often achieved. Creative, freed-up ways of thinking around problems lead to sophisticated solutions evolving; major breakthroughs are made and often powerful alliances are formed. The days when it was sufficient to be merely 'effective' are long gone. The dynamic of the future is one of collaborative endeavour, where the winners are going to be the teams that are most adaptive to the new ways of thinking and interacting. The biggest prizes will go to the people who are able to create the best additional value for all concerned.

NEGOTIATION ANSWERS

Check how many points you have scored in the exercise starting on page 84. The number following each **a**, **b** or **c** option is the score for that answer. The maximum score is 30. If you score 24–30, you're smart; 15–23, needs work but all is not lost; 14 or less, consider some training.

Question 1

a. 2   Not the best option for maximizing value, but if you have an interesting deal in the bag, do it. It's better than letting the other party walk away. A smarter negotiator would ask themselves what might be going on here.

b. 3   Why are you being offered more than you want? Find out what you have missed and re-evaluate. Maybe there is something you have overlooked and there could be more here than at first meets the eye. The first offer is never the best you can achieve. If it's of sufficient value to them to offer more, there is probably room for a little more negotiation.

c. 1   If you make it difficult, you might lose the deal altogether, and as the expert negotiator, it's you who has to take responsibility for your outcome. You are in danger of letting the sale slip through your fingers, let alone obtain maximum value.

Question 2

a. 2   If she agreed so readily, that's probably all she was expecting to achieve. You are most likely paying a little over the market value. Do some careful research and obtain a clearer picture of local market forces and the house itself.

b. 1   If you are putting in an offer and at the same time you are thinking it's a dodgy deal, you deserve all you get.

c. 3   She's willing to haggle: go for it! It may be that she was testing the water with her original price. It's for you to test in the other direction and see how much better a deal you could achieve.

Question 3

a. 1 Two years is a long time in business: anything could (and probably will) happen. Accept the job if you really want it, but don't have any expectations that what you are being promised will automatically appear.

b. 2 It's good that you believe in yourself, and that you should be remunerated properly for what you do. However, you leave yourself exposed and in danger of losing the opportunity. Better to share your thoughts and explore how you might help them reach your objective.

c. 3 If the job really is that great but they cannot (or will not) afford you, explore what is going on behind the scenes and how you might optimize the situation. Could they be going through temporary financial difficulties? Or perhaps they are not confident you will deliver on what you say? It's a great opportunity to arrive at a win-win outcome through some creative thinking.

Question 4

a. 3 Good. Get a dialogue going and see how you might accommodate their needs at minimum cost to yourself. Understand where their problems really lie. For example, could you help them reduce their logistics costs or other market challenges?

b. 2 It's the beginning of the downward spiral. They have you exactly where they want you. Sometimes market forces mean that you have to lower your price a little, but it's not a good place to be and you need to decide how you are going to protect your patch.

c. 1 What a wimp! In the words of Abraham Lincoln, 'Things may come to those who wait, but only the things left by those who hustle.'

Question 5

a. 1 Negotiation isn't your thing, is it? Learn to enjoy the game. If they find your price too high, the worst that can happen is they'll say no. You may be leaving many opportunities for finding extra value untapped.

b. 2 If you are pitching at only a little above your bottom line, you are too conservative: you are giving them all the value and creating none for yourself. Be more adventurous. Explore what else might be possible.

c. 3 The keyword is 'justify': you don't want to come across as crazy. So long as you can make an objectively compelling case for your fees, set the anchor high – you can always drop, if needs be. If you don't do it, they are certainly not going to do it for you!

Question 6

a. 1 A dangerous strategy: you cannot predict what might go wrong in the future. A seemingly small incident outside your control could endanger the whole financial security of your organization. A calculated risk is one thing – a bad gamble, something else entirely.

b. 2 You are not in business to put your profits at risk. Not all clients are worth retaining. If this one is worth keeping, they will talk some more and you will be able to arrive at a more effective solution.

c. 3 You understand your client's fears. Work the situation. You could agree a small penalty, but in return you want a higher base price or a bonus for early delivery, either of which will give you the resources you need to hire extra staff, and so ensure early delivery.

Question 7

a. 1 Don't you even want to know why? They are most likely gone for good and you have done nothing to stop them!

b. 3 Say that this gives you a new understanding of their needs. Could you reopen negotiations and offer them a new deal? Things are rarely as finalized as they might appear – especially if the prospect were to see something interesting.

c. 2 It may not be the price that is the issue: it could be higher quality, add-ons, delivery ... any number of things. Find out what the issue is and see if you can address it.

Question 8

a. 1 People make decisions based on how they feel. You need to get them on your side and only then can you bring in the numbers. While numbers can seem persuasive, they will usually mean much more to you than to other people. An understanding of what is going on for other people and how you could help them would be much more effective.

b. 3 It's best to drum up support on a personal basis. If people can see what's in it for them, and have already agreed to support your corner beforehand, you will find yourself in a strong position.

c. 2 It's good to get in there first and often helps you secure what you want, but it's not enough: you need to engage with people. The more they feel you could help them, the greater the chance of them reciprocating.

Question 9

a. 3 Your boss may not be happy, but will at least respect you for standing up for yourself. There is always room to give a little, say by delaying your departure or putting in some extra time beforehand.

b. 2 If it really is the holiday of a lifetime and means so much to you both, it's not something on which to compromise: you will probably regret it.

c. 1 Get a life! And some negotiation coaching! You have responsibilities at work, but you also have responsibilities at home – and to yourself.

Question 10

a. 2 Both parties need to feel they achieved what they want – but could there be more? The best negotiators see what else might be possible.

b. 1 If it's only about you, any success you may win will be shallow and very short-lived. Your future prospects don't look great.

c. 3 Each side has something the other wants, but if you explore around your interests it's often possible to build in more value for both parties.

TACTICS

TACTIC 7
BUILD YOUR TEAMS

The greatest forces are intangible.

NAPOLEON HILL

Surround yourself with talented people

Who are the key influential people in your life? Who is having a hand in scripting your future? What are the influences around you of which you might not even be aware?

The people, the thoughts, the ideas you surround yourself with all sculpt your life at both a conscious and an unconscious level. Sometimes we don't even notice what is going on. We absorb influences without thinking and they shape the person we are becoming until, as eminent life coach Fiona Harrold once so eloquently put it, 'You wake up one morning and exclaim, "Who is this stranger in my bed?" ' Your critical mind, the part of you that is consciously aware of your environment, is only part of the story of who you are. Much more powerful is what you are absorbing on the inside. It's your internal programming that causes you to think, act and respond in ways that are individual to you – and much of this programming comes from the people with whom you surround yourself.

Our friends and associates influence what we read, what we watch, what we wear, where we go, how we live … even what we think. And everything that we experience parks itself, like a tiny computer cookie, somewhere deep down, ready for our unconscious system to trigger it – sometimes at the most unexpected moments. Armed with this knowledge, you are well placed to start making more considered choices about the people you bring into your life, the people you work with, the teams you build around you and the people who could help you achieve your goals.

Recognize great qualities

Some of the teams you bring together might exist for just a matter of days, or even hours. Others will be with you for months or years as your journey unfolds. Nevertheless, as you start to make more informed choices about the people with whom you surround yourself, you will find yourself taking more control of the direction in which your life is heading.

Take a moment or two to consider the people who figure strongly in your life at present. What are the qualities in your associates that you admire and would like more of for yourself? What personal attributes and mindsets do you see in others that you find energizing and empowering? What is it that inspires you? What is it about these people that creates enriching experiences for you?

There are two reasons why it's important for you to explore these thoughts. First of all, by focusing on them you open up your subconscious to absorbing more of the same. You become more aware of how these qualities line up with your own values and aspirations, which allows you to zone in more instinctively on people and situations that give you more of what you want. You will also begin to see more clearly what is missing; what you need to bring into your life and work – the fresh thinking, the new ideas and perspectives.

A visionary organization hires people not just because of their capability to do a job, but because of who they are and how they will add to the evolving company culture and ethos. Visionary individuals look for people who have a verve and vitality of thinking that will enhance, develop and even challenge their own ways of thinking. Whether it's individuals, groups or whole organizations, when there's a dynamic meeting of minds and wills between focused people, sparks of renewed energy and creative spirit begin to fly. New ideas are born. Older concepts and practices are seen in a new light. New combinations of understanding begin to appear.

Push the boundaries

Be willing to push your boundaries in terms of the people you meet and the conversations you have. Who offers interesting insights? Who stimulates your creative spirit? Who can you learn from? Whose mind is filled with exciting possibilities?

As an elite performer you have the power not only to meet new opportunities, but also to create them on a daily basis. When you become clear about the kinds of people and events you want to attract into your life, you can set about making plans and taking the actions necessary to realize them. You will also be in a position to take control rather than simply letting things happen. Start to ask yourself:

- Which kinds of people do I want to have around me to stimulate ideas?
- Where do I find them?
- What are the conversations I need to have to move my plans forward?
- What do I have to offer such inspiring people in return?
- Are there people who could introduce me to others I want to meet?

Your power circles

Jim Rohn, one of the founders of modern personal development techniques, teaches that each one of us is the average of the five people we associate with most closely. This will reflect itself in your income, the way you dress, the way you think and what you do. What is it that motivates the people around you? How do they measure success and achievement? What is their level of income and wealth? What is the nature of their relationships? Who are their friends and associates? How do they show up in the world? All this is rubbing off on you, day after day ... and those computer cookies are stacking up.

Make a firm decision to surround yourself with people who are passionate about where they are going in life and about their vision of the future. Creative energy is infectious. When you start to reserve the space around you only for people whose life you would like to be living yourself, you will soon begin to realize just how valuable that space is to you. There are people who are energized by the idea that things are possible. There are imaginative people who seize life with zest and imagination, who are fun-loving and passionate about what they're doing and where they're going. People of this calibre will push you to reach your full potential because they themselves like to surround themselves with elite performers.

You may not notice changes within yourself straight away: they take a little while to get into your blood. However, as the weeks turn into months and you make considered choices on a regular basis, those around you will certainly start to notice. Be constantly aware of the values you want to surround you. Would you like to be making more money? Would you like to be more creative? Would you like to have more rewarding relationships? Would you like to travel more imaginatively? Would you like to have more adventure in your life and to push your boundaries further? Would you like to explore more of what might be possible?

In his book *Secrets of the Millionaire Mind*, T. Harv Eker says, 'Rich people admire other rich and successful people. Poor people resent rich and successful people.' Whether 'rich' for you means wealthy in material terms, or in terms of creativity, relationships, lifestyle, spirituality or anything else doesn't matter. It holds good for everything. Where do you belong?

It may be that there are people you need to ease out of your life. There may be negative people, people who criticize, people who suck energy and time out of you, people who are limiting you. They have their own life's journey; let them go with your blessing and good wishes. Your mission is to build around you a circle of people whose beliefs and values make you feel inspired and energized.

It takes all sorts

Each generation develops new outlooks and perspectives on life, so make sure you avoid being lured into the trap of restricting your power circle to particular generations, or groups or types of individuals. Jack Gardner says in his book *Words Are Not Things*, 'No one will lie to you more than your imagination.' It's all too easy to be wrapped up in your own way of thinking, reinforced by the goodwill of those around you, to build up ideas based on one set of views and to miss the opportunities that might come from thinking completely differently. Elite performers make sure they regularly draw a freshness and vitality of thinking into their environment. How many friends do you have who are considerably younger than you? How many friends do you have who are significantly older than you? No single generation has a monopoly on wisdom. There will always be streams of people with fertile, creative imaginations, people who will step up to the edge and ask what might be possible, people who want to know what's on the other side of the mountain and what the view is like from the top. Make sure you take your place among them. This is vitality at work.

Many top performers, including the CEOs of some of the largest, most profitable and highest-profile companies in the world, have a personal mentor or coach. Their meetings may be in person or over the phone, and are an opportunity to discuss, in a regular weekly time slot, progress towards goals, potential challenges, innovative ideas and so on. Sometimes we can be a little too close to a situation to see the facts objectively. Discussion with a coach or mentor can usefully give a different perspective. Increasingly, companies are introducing a similar resource for different levels of management as they realize how this accelerates progress.

> *We cherish not just what people do, but who they are. Not just who they are when they walk in through the door, but what made them who they are, the person they are all the time.*
>
> Indra Nooyi

It's all right to let go

All too often, people spend a great deal of time and energy building teams around them but then find it difficult to let those teams do what they should be doing. They hire people to do a particular job, but then still insist on doing key aspects of the work themselves. They demand perfection. They find it difficult to believe that anybody else could do it as well as they can, or that they can be trusted; they seem to find any one of a thousand reasons why they have to see to everything personally.

If you are one of these people, it is possible, of course, that you're right. It's highly likely that you would do whatever it takes – but at what price? It usually means that you are denying yourself the time and space to do the things that, genuinely, only you can do. It often also means you're not allowing your teams to perform to their full potential and add their personal contribution and value. As a result, you may become so involved in the nitty-gritty that you are unable to see the bigger picture or any other opportunities that might await you.

Let go! If someone else can do a job at least 80 per cent ... 75 per cent ... even 65 per cent as well as you can, let them do it. Most people, with support, guidance and, if necessary, training, usually grow into the responsibility given to them. Allow others to shine. It may well be they'll come up with ideas or ways of doing things that hadn't even occurred to you. Perhaps, over time, they will add even more value than you had considered possible. As H. Jackson Brown Jr says, 'Strive for excellence, not perfection.'

The big question is, of course, how do you let go? How can you give other people the responsibility, but still know that things will be all right? How do you know they will not bring about calamity?

The answer lies with you – in three ways.

First, remember you selected your team members and invited them to come on board. Trust your judgment. It's your responsibility, of course, to ensure that they are given all the resources they need in order to deliver what you want, which might include elements such as training, support, encouragement, physical resources, but then let them get on with it. Indeed, create an environment where it's a delight for them to do so. Remember that they are on your side. Numerous psychological studies of group interaction have shown that people naturally step out in front in areas where they feel confident and have particular expertise. For people with a track record of achievement, it's part of their nature to want to get things done.

Second, recognize that it's going to take a shift in your mindset to get you to start thinking on a bigger scale. You are going to need to develop some new beliefs about the people you work with. You know that if someone else were standing in your shoes, they would be looking at things a little

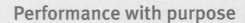

TACTICS IN ACTION

Performance with purpose

Indian-born Indra Nooyi is a business leader with a difference. She is often to be seen around her offices barefoot and wearing a sari, and singing in the halls. She wanted to attract into her company talent that would take them through tough trading times. She needed visionary players to match her own high expectations; players who wanted to work with passion; players who shared her commitment to ethical growth.

Indra Nooyi is the chief executive of PepsiCo, employing some 185,000 employees in almost 200 countries. She made it her mission to create an organization of individuals who espouse her beliefs and values, and who would build with her one of the best and most ground-breaking food companies in the world.

She coined the saying 'Performance with purpose' and, by building a company culture around making the world a better place (as well as generating revenue, of course), she has succeeded in attracting a wealth of sparkling young talent and capturing their loyalty. She wants forward-looking people, well versed in manipulating the latest advances in technology and digital thinking. She wants talent with a high emotional intelligence and with skills in relating to people in many different cultures and markets. She wants people committed to growing the company through planned sustainability and well-founded ethics, looking not only within the organization itself, but also at the ways it would do business in a wide variety of communities around the world. It is this relentless pursuit of excellence in her teams that lies at the core of her success.

Nooyi has developed a powerful understanding that success comes from building great internal and external partnerships and relationships at any level. She creates the opportunity for her employees to fulfil an important basic human need – the need to make a difference. She fosters an environment that encourages talented people to want to give their best because they are working on something they believe in. As a result, they feel empowered and have a deep personal commitment to the future growth and well-being of the company.

Nooyi says, 'We have to make sure that people who work for us are able not just to make a living but also to have a life.' And, in another interview, 'We want our employees to be thrilled to come to work every day.'

differently from you, so you know you can do it, too. Use the exercise on page 109 to help you become more skilled in this.

Third, just do it. Let go! You know you will always be able to step in at the last minute if you really need to. However, in the meantime, give people the space and encouragement to enable them to shine. Who knows where this might lead? One of the by-products of our technological age is that ever-increasing numbers of people love to express their creativity. Learn to live in anticipation, even awe, of what this might bring about. Think of yourself as the doting mother or father of your brood. What could happen if your teams were twice as big ... three times as big ... ten times as big? The growth of every great team and organization starts with one individual's vision and belief in their people. Could that be you?

As Arthur C. Clarke said in his book *Profiles of the Future*, 'The only way to discover the limits of the possible is to go beyond them into the impossible.'

Create a 'mastermind group'

As early as 1937, Napoleon Hill advocated the value of a group of like-minded individuals working together to help each other expand their potential.

> *When a group of individual brains are coordinated and function in harmony, the increased energy created through that alliance becomes available to every individual brain in the group.*
>
> Napoleon Hill, *Think and Grow Rich*

A 'mastermind group' is a group of peers who enjoy a synergy and mutual commitment to success and growth. They meet on a regular basis to sharpen up their skills, brainstorm and test out ideas, share wisdom and experience and create accountability structures. Little could Napoleon Hill have known when he was writing how effectively the notion would be harnessed by future generations. Today, in an era when knowledge is cheap, and it's the innovative use of knowledge and information that makes some people wildly successful and leaves others sitting on the sidelines, the power of collaborative thinking comes into its own. 'Thought leaders', the winners of the future, seek out what they require, adapt it, reshape it, make fresh connections of ideas and redefine new realities. The energized interaction of excited minds raises new questions and reframes challenges like never before. Focused serial achievers have learned to enhance their own resources by bringing together dynamic thinkers with a taste for success.

If you are interested in this self-support idea, seek out motivated, focused players who, like you, aspire to raise their game. Arrange to meet on a regular basis – say, once a month – with a clear objective, both to help and support each other as well as to hold each other accountable.

James Mapes, author of *Quantum Leap Thinking*, says:

> *The people you choose must be willing to persist, explore,*
> *give and take positive criticism without assuming a defensive*
> *posture, and be willing to listen. Above all, they must trust*
> *and be trusted. These are the people you can confide in, be*
> *vulnerable with, and be committed to. It is the chemistry of*
> *the group, its synergy, that provides the source of power for*
> *a quantum leap ... It is your brainpower multiplied.*

It's a tall order, but it can be a game-changing resource. Mark Victor Hansen and Robert Allen, writing in *The One Minute Millionaire*, advocate a three-month probationary period for each member to ensure you have the right people.

How often you meet will vary from group to group. Many mastermind groups meet once a month. My own group meets quarterly, as that allows time for each of us to achieve what we need to achieve. We usually meet for drinks and dinner in a restaurant, which also makes it a lively social

EXERCISE **SHIFT YOUR BELIEFS**

As a leader, a person of influence, you are going to need to strike an inspiring and motivating balance between working freely and collaboratively and directing the course you and your team will need to follow. The same is true whether you are thinking in terms of your career or business, or, in more general terms, about your life's direction. It falls to you to bring out the best in the people around you. As you probably suspect deep down, this could mean a little bit of a shift in some of your long-held beliefs. Spend one or two minutes thinking about each of the following questions in turn, and write down a few notes in response to each. Invest the time. If you run out of thoughts, just ask yourself, 'What else could I add here?' or 'Who could I draw inspiration from to discover something new?' You may surprise yourself when you see where you arrive.

1. What are the beliefs you currently hold about letting people take responsibility for outcomes?
2. What evidence do you use to support these beliefs?
3. What evidence could there be to the contrary?
4. In what ways do your current beliefs fail to serve your best interests?
5. What will happen if you continue to hold on to your current beliefs?
6. What could happen if you were able to believe the opposite?
7. In what ways are your present beliefs preventing your teams from reaching their full potential?
8. What more empowering beliefs could you hold?
9. Would you feel able to consent to adopting some or all of these more empowering beliefs?

occasion. We have fun, laugh and joke, but that never masks the serious-ness of our intent. We are all there because we value the input of our team members and the fact that we invariably come away invigorated and with a new slant on what each of us had been thinking and planning. What matters is the commitment to outcomes for every single member, and also a serious commitment to full participation. In my group, I can only ever remember one absence – and that was on account of an unexpected business crisis. Be ruthless over commitment. You owe it to yourself and to each other. Elite players perform at the very top of the league the whole of the time.

It's good to divide the meeting into two halves. In the first half, each person takes ten minutes to recount the value they took away from the pre-vious session, and reports on the action they took as a result. When you know you are accountable to a demanding group of friends, it focuses the mind wonderfully on what you need to have achieved in the intervening period! In the second half of the meeting, each member has ten to fifteen minutes to present anything on which they would like input from the rest of the group; the breadth and scope of thinking that a well-chosen group of peers can give rise to can often be breathtaking. Take copious notes: you won't remember it all.

Who's in the driving seat?

As you work on your personal growth you'll discover new ways for people to help you, new ways to engage and inspire your teams and new ways of working with others towards your goals and plans. This is equally true whether it concerns your career or business life, your personal relation-ships, your wealth, your sense of well-being, indeed any aspect of your life. The people you surround yourself with, the books you read, the places you frequent – these all help to shape who you are becoming, but you are the one who has the responsibility to make things happen around you. You are the individual who has created what you have achieved up until now and who has built the groups of people with whom you surround yourself.

You are the person who is going to do the thinking and take the actions that will fashion your future.

Remember your place as a leader. Make it your aim to leave every situation and every person better than you found them, every individual all the richer for having connected with you.

Let's now take a look in **Tactic 8** at how you can accelerate your outcomes by working with other people. What do you need to be thinking in order to raise the game? How can you optimize your connections for more inspired outcomes? Be bold in your expectations of what you might achieve.

As the Scottish mountaineer William Hutchison Murray declared (quoting Goethe), 'Boldness has genius, power and magic in it.'

TACTIC 8
INSPIRE CONFIDENCE

Sometimes all it takes is being able to see yourself differently.

KATHY FRESTON

Foster the power of teamwork

You have the power to inspire people to give you much more than you might believe. The results you have achieved so far with your teams are the outcome of your thinking, the consequences of how effectively you have communicated your ideas and of the actions you have taken. So far, so good. Let's imagine that you're going to use these results as a baseline for the future. You may have decided that the time has come to shift your outcomes to a whole new level; not just one shift, but a whole series of shifts over time that bring you accelerated success. You are going to sharpen up how you inspire your teams to deliver.

What could happen if not only you, but also the people you have chosen to surround yourself with, all started to show up as a dynamic powerhouse of innovation and creativity? How would it be if all of you together developed a deep inner commitment to performing with pure brilliance? People love strong leadership. If you are able to lead by example with passion, confidence and vision, the energy you create will become infectious.

As Einstein said, nothing happens until something moves. It falls to you, therefore, to make things happen, to set the wheels in motion in such a way that people feel compelled to strive for the best they can be – and then some. Great leaders have the ability not only to create major achievements for themselves and their organization, but also to release within each individual the potential for world-class performance, the ability to stand out and shine. Of course, there will be cynics who say it can't be done, and that people are too self-interested. That's fine. There are people for whom a lifetime of mediocrity is sufficient. There are people who will always be too scared to step up and make a difference. On the other hand, there are those who will choose to run with the notion that if you help people feel fulfilled and inspired, they will play their part in the unfolding action. These are people who generate possibility, and lead groups into action with visionary purpose and energy. Cream always rises to the top.

Inspire your teams

As people see how you open doors for them and add value to their life's journey, you will find it increasingly easy to inspire them. We all have a basic need to feel a sense of purpose, a belief that what we do makes a difference. If you are the person who creates new understanding, new combinations of thoughts for those around you, you will be well on the way to building a basis for trust and confidence. It may be that you can open up for them new opportunities with regard to their personal dreams and ambitions. It might be that you create for them a sense of being part of something bigger than they can be on their own. It could be a sense of satisfaction in sheer excellence that touches their lives deep down ...

People's commitment to a vision can come from a wide range of different sources, but fundamentally it stems from an emotional buy-in. It's human nature to make decisions at an emotional level, then to ratify them with logic. It's when people want something that they begin to need it. Make it your job to plant the seeds of desire and aspiration – and to nurture them. Take the time to find out what pushes people's buttons. Show people that you care! As Theodore Roosevelt said:

> *No one cares how much you know, until they know how much you care.*

Robin Sharma, coach to some of the world's top CEOs, has a persuasive take on it in his book *The Leader Who Had No Title*:

> *... sustained change only happens when we shift at an emotional rather than at a logical level. I wanted to get under your skin and touch your heart rather than just speak to your head. You can hear a good idea one hundred times and fail to make it a piece of who you are until you experience it viscerally – in your body. Only then does it rise from being just some idea to a truth to you.*

▶ PAGE 117

EXERCISE **THE BIGGER YOU**

Use this exercise daily to grow within yourself a sense of expanded potential. As you work on it you will feel yourself becoming more empowered, more self-assured and better equipped to lead those around you. Read it through a few times so you know what to do, then find a quiet, comfortable spot where you won't be disturbed for fifteen to twenty minutes. Allow plenty of time: this is an opportunity to create a special experience. Some people like to play soft, gentle music in the background, but it's not essential.

Sit in a relaxed but alert position and start to concentrate on your breathing: in ... and out ... and in ... and out. Take your time ... slowly ... gently ... As you become more relaxed, you may wish to let your eyelids close.

Imagine you are standing looking straight ahead. Another person appears before you, but, strangely, they look almost like you – almost. Somehow they seem to be ever so slightly different, but you can't quite put your finger on it. Maybe they stand just a touch taller. Perhaps they are a little broader in the shoulders. Is it their smile or the look in their eyes that is just that bit more engaging? What strikes you most is the poise, the air of self-assurance, the charisma that seems to emanate from them.

Feel yourself gently drift out of your body and into the other you. Step inside the other you and make yourself comfortable. You were right: it does feel like you, except there somehow seems to be more space. You stretch your shoulders, pull yourself up to your full height, stretch your fingers, expanding to make full use of the space inside your new body. It's an empowering sensation.

As you become comfortable in your new body, you start to look through the new eyes and realize you are seeing the world a little differently. You are looking with a quietly composed inner strength, which means nothing can faze you any more. Everything just seems so easy. You feel a great sense of purpose and, as people approach you, there is an immediate rapport. Everyone seems to sense your great care for them and they in turn want to help you all they can. Wherever you look, life seems full of opportunities. You enjoy the sensation of a deep, quiet inner confidence, and you know that your vibrant inner strength generates momentum for others to perform at their best.

Take some time just to enjoy the feelings. Ask yourself what you really like about them. What pleases you most? If there were something that you wish might last for ever, what would it be? Drink the whole experience in like a rare, fine wine and allow it to stream through to every cell of your body. Feel a warm glow run through you and a surge of strength and confidence course through your veins. You feel empowered, focused and motivated.

The finger squeeze

At the height of the experience, when you have taken time to build up the state, take your middle finger and thumb on each hand, gently squeeze them together and hold for a few moments.

Gather up the thoughts and feelings that you are going to want to take back with you and keep for the future as you prepare to return to your body. When you are ready, gently start to drift back to your own body. You will find it a bit of a tight squeeze now, so you will have to stretch in every direction in order to accommodate this new way of experiencing life that you've brought back with you. You've become aware of how much bigger and more expansive life could feel for you. Take a moment when you've arrived back and, when you're ready, open your eyes.

For a few moments, clear your mind: maybe remind yourself what you had for breakfast yesterday or what you did last Saturday afternoon. Then, once again, squeeze together the middle finger and thumb of each hand. As you squeeze, you will find the state of mind you have created coming back.

Just as when you squeezed your left knee in **Tactic 1**, you have created a trigger that you can use to feel empowered, confident and courageous. Repeat the exercise daily to maintain and build your inner power.

Become the leader others look to

Make it a habit to work on your inner strength and energy every day. Here is my secret strategy. Every morning I get up early and spend an hour on my personal growth. I meditate, I plan, I work out what I need to do in order to arrive at the results I want within my set timescales, I read inspirational books. It's 'exceptional me' time, reserved purely for my own development and growth. Day by day I build a great storehouse of resources to draw on, resources built on the achievements of the best thinkers and leaders I can find. Week after week, month after month, my storehouse has emerged like a great fortress, built stone by stone. Each day I take stock of my progress and remind myself to push my boundaries and raise the bar. Over time it has become, for me, a way of thinking that is at the very core of how I operate.

On one occasion, it started with a very potent question from Robin Sharma:

> What five things need to happen in the next twelve months in order for this to be your best year yet?

Robin's question created a time frame in which I was to measure my achievements; it unleashed a flood of thoughts about what my potential might turn out to be. I started regularly easing myself into the 'bigger me', as you have done in the exercise on pages 115–16. I also pushed myself to ask how I could seek more effective and enduring help from my teams. I was focused on building sustainable growth for all of us. We are on life's journey together, and creative energy comes into its own when we can bounce thoughts, plans and actions off each other. This was me taking responsibility for myself.

Authors of *Cracking the Millionaire Code* Mark Victor Hansen and Robert G. Allen note how regular attention to personal growth lies at the very heart of outstanding performance:

When you stretch your brains, your body, and your being,
a sacred space is created for receiving enlightened ideas
destined to change your world and the world around you.
Thus prepared, you're more highly sensitive to the best ideas –
more aware of the opportunities hidden all around you.

This practice builds a deep-rooted ethical confidence and self-assurance that inspires people to respond to you and with you. Confidence is sexy. (Not to be confused with arrogance, which is distinctly unsexy!) People love strong leadership. It's about empowering other people to rise to their own peaks of greatness. It's about making possible things that might have previously seemed impossible, or at least very difficult. It's NOT, I repeat, NOT about ego! If you think your ego is in any danger of becoming tangled up in this, check you have parked it at the door. After lack of vision and lack of discipline, ego is the single biggest factor that gets in the way of great achievement. Your underlying motivation must be one of service and a desire to let other people look to you for their strength and motivation. Think charisma. Think inspiration. Think deep inner wisdom and capability.

You will find that, as people see the integrity of your approach, your sense of vision and your unshakeable commitment to superb outcomes, you will be touching and influencing the heart of their beliefs and values. They will become more of who they really are. They will often start to explore more of their own potential and expand, entering into energized thinking. We all want to grow, flourish and prosper, even if these concepts mean different things to different people.

Many organizations throughout the world are increasingly coming to understand the effectiveness of leadership through inspiration. They are realizing that, rather than micro-managing their staff, it is much more effective to create an empowering culture where teams have the opportunity to develop their own thinking and grow their potential. Google, for example, allows its staff to spend one day of the working week on their own projects

Inspire results and have fun

Pete Carroll glanced at the feature in the *Los Angeles Times* with a big grin. 'Today he's the best coach in the country, the perfect man for a perfectly impossible job,' he read. It hadn't always been like that. He remembered coming to Los Angeles three years earlier to take up the job of head coach of the University of Southern California Trojans football team – amid much opposition from the press. He was the fourth choice, the other three potentials each having declined the position. His reputation wasn't great, though it was well known how hard the New York Jets played for him. He'd been excited by the prospect of turning the Trojans' fortunes around.

Within thirteen months the team had achieved nineteen wins in twenty games and Carroll had captured his players' passion, ferocious commitment and pride. One report recounts how he fired up his players in a team meeting: 'We own this city when we do it right, boys, and it's huge. It's LA! Hollywood! It's all that. It's the Trojans ...!' The atmosphere was electric. He didn't mind people watching his training techniques or fear that they might steal his training secrets. He knew how to inspire results, and that was what mattered most.

Carroll had achieved his results through a keen understanding that players respond to coaching most effectively through the activity and language that they know best themselves. He'd run everywhere during practice, be right in the middle of drills and, at the same time, have at least one junior member of staff playing catch with him. It was a dynamic, high-energy, high-focus experience each time. He drove with emotional involvement, but each training session had to have space for fun, too, with laughter, buffoonery, music and dancing. Knowing that a championship game whizzes past at lightning speed if you're a player, he pushed his men harder than they would ever encounter in the game itself, but he also recognized the motivational power of fun. As they left the locker room for the game, he'd say, 'Let's keep the fun going because this is serious.' He would make it a thrilling experience.

The formidable relationship Carroll built with his team, and the strong philosophy of intense competitiveness, empowerment and growth, transformed the USC Trojans from a team in steep decline to a magnificently cohesive unit of talented, successful players.

and ideas. New concepts are born, creativity flourishes, fresh connections are made and these organizations appreciate that their future competitive edge lies in the freedom of thought that they espouse. Teams are happier because they have the space to flex their wings and explore untapped potential. This is new-generation elite thinking in action.

Make the most of tough times

When times are tough we're pushed to be more resourceful in our thinking. That's when outstanding leaders emerge and show their true colours. Welcome challenging opportunities, because it's when the going gets tough that you have the chance to shine and really make your mark. It's at such times that those who have built up their inner resources step out in front. It's not enough to be good; everyone can be good. It's not even enough to be excellent; the competition is too fierce.

As the legendary comedian Steve Martin once said, 'Be so good they can't ignore you.' There is a profound truth in this statement, which is applicable to virtually any life situation. Martin was determined to make it to the top of his profession and developed techniques and methods for audience control that have long outlived his stage career. He shares many of these in his autobiography, *Born Standing Up*.

We live in an intensely competitive world, and it is only going to become more so. The knack to thriving in this environment is to be seen to perform with elegant ease, and to deliver outcomes better than anybody else. When faced with difficult times, think of them as a gym for the mind. It's your opportunity to work up your creative thinking and power through. This means that when things get back to 'normal', you will be stronger, leaner and fitter than those who merely struggled through. It will then become much easier for you to deliver a superb performance. Once you are comfortable with your personal development and growth, you will find that it's not difficult to be the best: you simply need to be that little bit better than everybody else.

Small can be beautiful

Swimmer Michael Phelps took the world by storm at the 2008 Beijing Olympics when he won race after race to achieve eight gold medals and the record for the most gold medals won in a single Olympics. Yet, take a look at these numbers:

2.32	0.08	1.89	0.67	5.14	2.29	0.01	0.13

These are the numbers of seconds by which Phelps won in each of the finals. Most of the differences were tiny, but they were enough to establish him as the world's best swimmer. He said of his success:

> *When you have an Olympic gold medal it stays with you for ever. It never gets old listening to your national anthem with a gold medal around your neck.*

It's the same for you; the margin that sets you apart doesn't have to be huge. However, as you establish yourself as an elite performer, people will be beating a path to your door, clamouring for a piece of the action. Realign your thinking patterns to those of world-class performers. Leaders emerge through powerful, innovative thinking – and that can so easily be you!

Be innovative

Innovative thinking comes about when you start making unusual connections between ideas. Think back for a moment to our discussions about modelling successful people in **Tactic 2**. As you work on this you will develop a unique collection of ideas, methods and approaches drawn from the best of the best of those you admire – together with your own unique life experiences. What could happen if you took one part of someone's brilliant idea that you have squirrelled away, and used it in an entirely different context? Maybe after a bit of thought you might add a little of something from a different source. Keep asking yourself, 'Out of all the resources I have at my disposal, what might work effectively in this situation? What combination of thoughts might create a great outcome?' The more you do this, the more easily you will find innovative questions popping into your mind. Be open to making unusual connections. Be willing to use nuances of ideas as you mix and match. Get used to looking for new ways of arriving at solutions – that's when it becomes exciting.

You do who you are

If you are to be successful as an inspirational leader, you are going to need to win (and keep) people's confidence. People will believe in you and follow you when they feel that you have their best interests at heart. They must know that you are the one who will help them to achieve their hopes and desires. They need to know instinctively that you share their beliefs and values and that you have a personal commitment to act on them in their interest. You must be able to connect with them, to relate to them and to their hopes and aspirations.

In **Tactic 2** we looked at how you 'walk the walk'. As you establish your leadership credentials, this will really come into its own. Everything you do should reflect the integrity of who you are. People need to see that your behaviour is a continuation of your thoughts and words. How people see you will determine how they'll respond.

I wonder, for example, if you can remember seeing a manager in an organization ask their staff to do things or behave in a certain way, then felt surprise when you saw the manager behave as if the same rules didn't apply to them? What were the thoughts that went through your mind? What might the staff have been thinking? How effectively did that organization function?

There are managers and there are leaders. Leaders are the people who inspire trust, respect and loyalty – and they do so through the perceptions they create. Leaders act in accordance with what they say, and deliver on what they said they would do. If you say it, you do it! No ifs, no buts, no maybes. Excuses are for losers and also-rans. People around you respond to the evidence of their eyes and ears. Over time, the constant stream of successful cause-and-response sequences forms the basis of trusting relationships. This is equally true in our business relationships, our social environment, our private relationships – indeed in whatever we do.

Vast numbers of people around the globe plod through life in a state of silent inertia. They suffer mediocre managers and mediocre relationships because they can't muster the energy or courage to change their situation. And they muddle along with a constant niggling background pain, a pain that is caused by their inability to connect and build strong, trusting partnerships.

It needn't be like this. Barefoot Doctor, writing in his *Handbook for the Urban Warrior*, invites people who find themselves in such situations to take action and trust themselves to choose a new direction that will lead to a path of healthy growth:

> *Trusting yourself requires that you exercise your power of discrimination, which arises from deep within your belly ...*
> *When you're with someone or in a situation where your chest feels tight and you have a nagging sense of unease in your gut ... get away from there and don't waste any time about it.*

Your role as an individual who makes things happen is the other side of the coin. Make sure you work hard at earning people's trust and confidence. Make it your mission to create so much reason for people to believe in you and trust you that they passionately want a piece of your action. That's how powerful teams grow and prosper. You need to take responsibility for making it happen through everything that you do; there is no room for half-measures. Be ready to help people perform at their best. Show them you have their best interests at heart. Be ready, too, to show them you care, to show them your appreciation with all sincerity, and to congratulate them when they shine.

How will people see things?

You have an unbelievable capacity to influence and inspire confidence – if you only choose to recognize it and exercise it. As you work on building your sphere of powerful influence, you will become increasingly aware of how important great communication is in achieving what you want. Communication is the art of creating a compelling message and taking control of how effectively you are understood. How people perceive your message has a direct bearing on how they act on it. You can 'pre-frame' your message to reach more resourceful outcomes. You can consciously build better rapport as you communicate. You can measure the response you are receiving and tailor your message accordingly. The more adept you are at controlling your communications, the better your outcomes will be.

In **Tactic 9**, we look at how the great communicators make things happen.

TACTICS IN ACTION

Share values, beliefs and dreams

Michael Rubin is the founder and CEO of GSI Commerce, an online shopping fulfilment centre employing up to ten thousand people at peak times. When the opportunity arose for him to do a television programme for CBS, involving him going undercover as a seasonal worker in his own company, he jumped at the chance, much to the amusement of his board of directors. He became Gary Rogers and, for a week, worked alongside the people who made his company what it is. His mission was to see how his teams were working and how productivity could be improved.

The experience turned out to be rather more than he had bargained for. He loaded a delivery truck with another seasonal worker, Rashelle, and injured her with a box in the process. He worked alongside Michelle and was astonished to see how she had devised her own procedure for scanning labels and sorting parcels that increased her own productivity by 25 per cent per hour compared to her fellow operatives. He worked alongside Adam in the complaints department and was inspired by how it seemed, as he put it, to be 'in his DNA to tackle difficult situations and get great outcomes'. He worked alongside Shannon, packing orders, and not only failed to make the speed required, but also messed up some of the boxes he was packing. He was fired from his own company.

Gary, as he was now known, also connected with the people he was working with. He shared in the tragedy of Adam's daughter, who had died at birth; in the toughness of life for Shannon, who was working seven days a week to raise her two boys; in the exuberance of order picker Cameron, who had lived on the streets between the ages of fifteen and seventeen and now appreciated the second chance he was being given in life. He was inspired by the passion and commitment of the people he met.

When Rubin eventually revealed who he was, his co-workers were bowled over – especially when he showed his appreciation in very practical ways. One was promoted and sent for training; another received money for her son's football league. Rubin showed the video of his experiences to the whole company and thanked them for all they were doing to make the company a success. The humanity and care they saw in their boss blew them away. They saw him share in their values, beliefs and dreams. The outcome for company morale was phenomenal.

TACTICS

TACTIC 9
COMMUNICATE FOR RESULTS

*The most important thing in communication is to
hear what isn't being said*

PETER DRUCKER

Be a person of influence

How do you become a powerful communicator? How do you win over people to your ideas? How do you come to be a person who understands what others need to hear and proceeds to inspire them to action?

Great communication lies at the very heart of success, both in terms of what you say overtly and in the messages you give out in other ways. HOW you say something is at least as important as what you say. You might have the best ideas, the most well-thought-out, logical plans, but if you are unable to connect with people's emotions, you are unlikely to bring your ideas to fruition together.

Understanding your message is only part of the story. What's much more important is a reason to engage with it. You need to be the motivator who will push their buttons, the catalyst who will inspire people to take action. The quality of your message will determine the response you receive. The art of great communication lies in knowing how to piece together the various elements into a powerful message.

Patricia Martin, in her book *RenGen: Renaissance Generation*, has coined the evocative phrase 'catalytic people' – people who have ground-breaking ideas and who have the ability to engage the hearts and minds of those around them to create a shift in mindset and attitude. It's as much about inspirational communication as it is about the ideas themselves.

Getting the knack

Some people seem to be born communicators. The right words just seem to flow easily for them, and it's impressive to see how people respond as they wish them to with barely an effort on their part. For most of us, though, it's an acquired art – and one that can be learned. Just as athletes perform various exercises to hone their skills and build particular sets of muscles, so you too can train yourself to have a strong impact through what you say and how you say it.

The secret to great communication is to understand that only a small part of it happens at a conscious level – what we normally see and hear. It's what happens 'below the surface' that makes the most impact and brings about outcomes. Whether the outcome is good or adverse depends on the delivery. Experts say only 7 per cent of the outcome derives from the words we say; 55 per cent comes from body language and eye contact, and 38 per cent comes from tonality – vocal tone, speed, pitch, volume. Use this knowledge to your advantage by planning what you say and how you say it. As a result, you will feel much more in control of situations. You will also be more likely to achieve the outcome that you want. You will learn to create a context for the other person to understand your message better.

When we address the unconscious mind we can influence people's attitudes and behaviours very quickly. The management psychologist Duane Lakin notes:

> It is not what we say that makes a difference. It is how we say it and how it is received. Words create action but only if they are engineered to do so.

Taking responsibility for how your message is received is powerful. It means that you plan what you want the other person (or group of people) to think and feel as a result of what you have to say. Elite performers plan what they want to be understood and then deliver accordingly. They take control of the message and make sure it is received as they intend.

How do they need to hear it?

When communicating with someone, many people make the cardinal mistake of forgetting that what they need to concentrate on is actually not what they want to say, but what the other person is hearing. World-class communicators have a great strategy to make sure their message is heard.

The human mind processes the information it receives in four different ways. These help us create a context in the light of our previous experiences in life, our values and our beliefs. These are described as:

visual   auditory   kinaesthetic   auditory digital

Visual people interpret information by seeing it. Auditory people, on the other hand, make better sense of what they hear rather than what they experience visually. Kinaesthetic people are more 'hands on' and form opinions by handling things and going on 'gut feel', while the auditory digitals like to think issues through.

Although we all use aspects of all of these at different times, everybody has a natural preference, just as we might prefer certain types of sporting activity, food or colour. We use these preferred modes of understanding to form our personal impressions. Can you think of a time, for instance, when you were explaining something to someone using 'auditory' terms – 'heard him say ... called on ... loud and clear ...' – and they just weren't 'getting it'? Then you switched to visual terms (for argument's sake) – 'the way I saw it ... it looked like ... mental image ...' – and they understood it straight away.

People often reveal their preferred modes of understanding through key words that they use. Here is a response that might be given by four different people to the same situation:

- I **see** what you mean.
- I **hear** what you say.
- I'm **getting a handle** on what you're saying.
- I **understand** your point.

We throw these sorts of phrases around liberally, without too much thought. Yet to the alert observer they provide valuable insights into how the individual's subconscious mind operates – and therefore how to access their

TACTICS IN ACTION

What do they need to know?

A train crash is rarely great PR for a railway company. Therefore, when an innovative tilting 'Pendolino' train, the fastest and newest type of train operating in the UK, crashed in a remote region of Cumbria on its way from London to Glasgow in February 2007, it presented a very particular challenge to the head of Virgin Trains, Sir Richard Branson.

Sir Richard is a charismatic leader and talented communicator. On hearing about the crash, he abandoned his holiday in Switzerland and travelled to the scene of the accident. Of the 120 passengers on board, one was killed and more than twenty had been injured. Speaking to the press at a safe distance from the overturned carriages, he made a number of key points that give great clues to how an insightful communicator plans his message.

He said, 'The first thoughts of Virgin Trains are with the families and loved ones of those who have lost their lives or been injured in this terrible accident. We will do whatever we can to offer assistance in the days ahead.'

He eloquently praised the heroism of his driver, Iain Black, who was among the injured, because he stayed at his post. He said, 'The Pendolino performed brilliantly. We transport many millions of passengers and have spent a lot of money on Pendolinos. If you are going to have a massive accident, a Pendolino is the safest train to be in. The train itself stood up remarkably well; it's built like a tank. If this had been an old train, the injuries would have been horrendous. Pendolinos have solid crumple zones and most people managed to walk away.'

While acknowledging the accident, he highlighted the safety of his trains and the bravery of his driver. He took a very clear personal stake in everything that had happened, of the whole scenario, and praised everyone who played a part in it. He also went to visit the injured in hospital.

The empathic message he conveyed was a masterly lesson in handling a catastrophic situation and in focusing attention on the positive elements. The train driver hero story dominated the media. The crucial factor is to plan in advance the effect you want your message to have.

understanding. In a sales situation, for example, using language that the prospective client is most attuned to can fast-track a discussion to the next level – simply by using language that matches the prospect's.

Get used to listening out for the words and phrases that a person uses and then use similar expressions yourself in your interactions with them. Take your time as you listen. Create space. Remember, most people, as soon as they start a conversation, are all too keen to pour out whatever it is that they have to say with scant regard for the consequences. Instead, learn to value the opening moments as time that you can use both to set the tone of the dialogue and to gather as much information as you can to help you shape your message.

The table on the next page offers some suggestions for the types of phrases you might use when you have established the other person's preferred mode of understanding. As a rule of thumb, in the developed world it's estimated that 40 per cent of the population respond most to visual ideas, 40 per cent to kinaesthetic, with the other two information processing styles split evenly between the remaining 20 per cent. When you are speaking one-to-one with someone or in a small group, you will soon be able to identify their preferred modes of understanding. When speaking to a large group, or if you cannot identify people's preferred modes (say, when writing and you don't know who your reader is), use language from all four preferences in equal measure to help your message register.

Once you become adept at accessing people's preferred modes of understanding, you may become interested in more sophisticated ways of using language to influence people. If promotions are in prospect, what could you say to the decision makers to help focus attention on you as the preferred candidate? If you want to clinch a business deal, how could you help your prospect to forget about your competitors? If you want others to follow your way of thinking about a project, what seeds of ideas could you sow? How could you find words that accelerate the outcomes you want? Investigate the Smart Words section in the members' area of www.tactics4talent.com.

Visual	Auditory
How does it look to you?	How does that sound to you?
Illustrate what I mean	In a manner or speaking
Look into it	Loud and clear
Let me show you	Let's talk about it
Mental picture	Call on
Imagine this	Purrs like a kitten
I see what you mean	Rings a bell
In the light of	Echo your sentiments
In view of	I hear what you say
Shows signs of	Sounds familiar
Kinaesthetic	**Auditory digital**
How does it feel to you?	What's your opinion?
What would be the impact?	Have you considered?
Cool, calm, collected	I appreciate your concerns
In the heat of the moment	An interesting process
Get hold of	Great benefits
Go for it	Imagine the possibility
Razor sharp	Evaluate the options
A tough cookie	Decide what works
It boils down to	Motivate them
You can get a feel for	Estimate the potential

Influential listening

A great tool to improve the effectiveness of your communication lies in the quality of your listening. There is nothing quite so flattering to someone as focused, engaged listening. Yet so often in conversations we see people spending the moments between what they say simply planning their next volley of words rather than listening to the other person. When we listen – that is really, really listen – we are conveying to the other person the message that what they have to say is important, that we value what they have

▶ PAGE 135

EXERCISE DISCOVER SECRETS PEOPLE GIVE AWAY

Often we give away information about ourselves to other people without even being aware we are doing so. Use this exercise to explore what you might be giving away, and then learn to spot similar information being revealed by other people. It's important here that you follow the instructions as you read them. Avoid the temptation to read on ahead. You will obtain the best results just by responding naturally and immediately, but try to answer as fully as you can.

Question 1:
Think back to yesterday morning. What did you have for breakfast?

Stop at this point until you have answered the question.

Question 2:
Can you imagine your boss in a straitjacket and having green hair?

Again, stop at this point until you have considered the question.

As you thought about the questions, did you notice your eyes move? When we are thinking about something, our eyes naturally make small, involuntary movements. For right-handed people, the eyes tend to move to their left when they are remembering things and to their right when they are 'constructing' or imagining things. (The reverse usually applies for left-handed people.) Start to notice which way people's eyes move as they speak.

This is a great tool in negotiations. If someone is telling you how much better a deal they could obtain from a competitor of yours, or is explaining something else they want you to believe, and their eyes shift to their right, ask yourself what is going on. Are they remembering it? Or are they making it up?

▶ PAGE 134

Now go and practise. Install yourself in a café with a coffee or a pot of tea and observe people's conversations. (Be careful to do it from a safe distance or you might upset people.) Are they right-handed or left-handed? Are they remembering or are they imagining?

You can also deduce people's preferred modes of understanding from their eye movements:

- Visual: eyes move to the side and up.
- Auditory: eyes move to the side and level.
- Kinaesthetic: eyes move to the side and look down.
- Auditory digital: eyes invariably move to the left and also look down.

You cannot tell WHAT someone is thinking, but you can tell HOW they're thinking and plan your behaviour accordingly. This is, of course, how 'mind readers' practise their art. The human body naturally gives out lots of tiny involuntary signals. Use the opportunity to glean as much information as you can and tailor your message accordingly. It sounds more complicated than it actually is.

After a little practice you will soon find yourself thinking, for example, 'Ah, here's a visual person. I need to use "seeing" words', or 'Here's an auditory person, so I need to use "sound" words', and so on. As you explore more, you may begin to notice someone's muscles tightening slightly when all is not as it seems, or their skin becoming a little more shiny as you build a rapport. It's a fascinating aspect of human behaviour to study.

to say. No matter who, we each have our song to sing, our message that needs to be heard. Be generous in creating a space for them to be heard.

When we listen and show that we understand, that is when genuine communication takes place. We don't have to agree with what the other person is saying; we just have to make it possible for the other person to feel that they have shared their message effectively and that we care.

This was recently brought back home to me very effectively when I was trying to arrange some insurance. I was attempting to sort out a policy that is slightly unusual, but not completely outrageous. I called three well-known brokers and each one in turn asked me politely how they could help. I proceeded to explain what I wanted and why. In each case I hadn't finished speaking before the 'specialist' butted in and told me at length exactly what I needed – which bore little relation to what I actually wanted! At the end of each of the three conversations I felt unheard, my needs were left unmet and the insurance policy remained unsold. Their inability to 'listen' lost each of them probably around £10,000 in commission over the life of the intended policy – because they couldn't keep their mouths shut!

Most people in business would shrug their shoulders and move on. But suppose that happened just once a week for each of those brokers? How much business were they losing simply because they did not know how to listen? In reality, it doesn't happen on a weekly basis. Astonishingly, it happens on a daily basis across the world. Again and again and again! As the author of *Words Are Not Things*, Jack Gardner, says, 'Do not ask questions until you have trained yourself not to know the answers.'

Suppose you devoted just one conversation a week to deeply attentive listening, and as a result achieved a positive outcome you might not have otherwise achieved; it could be in business, it could be in a personal relationship – the principles are the same. Suppose you then extended this to one conversation a day. Suppose it could become the way you operate instinctively ... When you get used to listening closely, you will be astonished at what you are able to achieve, because the other person will feel

EXERCISE ASSESS YOUR PERFORMANCE

Here's how to sharpen up your performance as a communicator. Take a significant conversation you have had with someone recently and give yourself a score out of five for how well you did in each of the following:

- ☐ Decided you are going to be a superb listener in this conversation.
- ☐ Focused exclusively and wholly on the speaker.
- ☐ Maintained appropriate eye contact.
- ☐ Observed the speaker's body language.
- ☐ Listened for and absorbed the preferred communication style.
- ☐ Nodded, smiled and used receptive facial expressions.
- ☐ Encouraged the speaker by saying, for example, 'Yes', 'Uh-huh', 'Really?', 'What did you do then?'
- ☐ Asked closely relevant questions to clarify points.
- ☐ Refrained from adding similar experiences of your own, or interrupting.
- ☐ Been open, honest and respectful.
- ☐ Tuned out your own thoughts.
- ☐ Set aside judgments.
- ☐ Understood the key points enough to teach them to someone else.

Check your scores for impartiality. If a fierce rival was observing, would they have to concede that your scores are valid? Now select your two weakest scores and decide how to improve your performance in those areas.

A tall order? With a little practice, all of these skills will become second nature. Used together, they will make you a captivating listener. People who apply these listening skills are often described as wonderful conversationalists. Yet sometimes they barely utter a word. When you have learned the secret, it's that easy to control the perceptions you create!

that you have heard and understood, and will respond. They will experience your validation that what they have to say matters – and that really pushes people's buttons.

Your body language

Consider what secrets and messages about yourself you might be giving away, possibly without realizing that you're even doing so.

Ask yourself whether you look the part. Do you look like someone who is confident and would be described by others as an elite performer? The moment people set eyes on you, they form a first impression of who you are. You communicate with them subliminally before you have said a single word. Then, as you interact, the other person picks up more and more clues about who you are (as you pick up clues about them, too). So how do you bring these subconscious messages under control? How do you ensure that you are sending out only the messages of a successful, engaging individual?

Think yourself into 'your part' before you start your conversation, so that you can take control of how you want to come across. You have already learned a technique to help you 'step inside the skin' of another person. Use this technique and start to notice now how you look from somebody else's point of view as you play the part. Stand tall (on both feet!) and with your legs just slightly farther apart than feels natural. The strong stance will give you a feeling of confidence. Likewise, when sitting, sit tall and occupy ample space: avoid huddling.

In your conversation make frequent eye contact for the length of time and frequency that the other person finds comfortable. Research has shown that frequent eye contact inspires a feeling of trustworthiness and sincerity, as well as confidence. Avoid looking down – it gives the impression of weakness. Keep your head straight – a tilting head suggests you are looking for approval – and when you move your head do so slowly and smoothly. Remember, you are a person of substance.

Be 'present' in the conversation. Let your face be animated with expressions and let comfortable gestures add another level of expression to what you say. Many people have problems keeping their hands under control. The knack is to keep your arms bent at the elbows and your hands clasped gently in front. Then let your gestures flow out from this position to amplify the points that you make. Alternatively, let your arms hang loose by your sides and hold your index and middle fingers and thumb together lightly so that you don't fidget – it's a sign of a lack of confidence. Avoid gestures from the side: bring your hands in front first and then use the gesture to emphasize your point. Remember, too, to keep your hands out of your pockets. Watch out for any ticks or mannerisms (for example, touching your face, scratching your nose ... or worse!).

When you move, be conscious of how you present yourself to the world. Walk with a purposeful stride, but never rush. Successful people are people who are in control of their lives, and therefore they have no need to rush.

It's important that, no matter what you think about your situation, you convey the image of someone who is self-assured and has a sense of presence, while at the same time being warm and approachable, and also someone who is fun to be with. Observe how other successful people carry themselves and emulate them. When you take control of your physiology, it will give a constant feedback to your subconscious and help you deliver what you desire as the person you need to be. It will amplify the quality of your message.

The power of communication

The leadership coach John Baldoni observes:

> Communication is the glue that holds an organization together. It is the means by which we exchange ideas, learn from each other and, perhaps most importantly, connect to each other.

Great communication is the cornerstone of extraordinary relationships, extraordinary business, extraordinary collaboration and extraordinary results. It's an exchange of energy – and control over the quality of that energy is within your grasp. Think of a time when you ha such a rapport with someone that the air around you was supercharged with creativity as you bounced ideas around, where you were both on sparkling form and potently inspired by each other, where the connection was vibrant and electric. You have the power to recreate that again and again, whenever you want, through careful listening, through the language that you choose and through your body language.

Often, when we have experienced such a situation, it seems that everything just fell into place at the right time: the people, the circumstances, the respective backgrounds, the inspiration ... World-class performers understand that they have the power to create such outcomes at will – and are willing to use that power! They allocate time to learning how to read people and how to build those powerful connections. They arm themselves with techniques that enable them to put other people at ease and feel comfortable. The people they speak with feel inspired; they feel charmed and moved to respond in similar ways. Powerful relationships are built with extraordinary speed. Great business deals are closed more easily. Inspired career moves seem to appear from nowhere. Interesting opportunities arise. Things begin to fall into place!

By taking control of how you communicate, you create a formidable accelerator to your progress.

TACTIC 10
COMMIT TO CHANGE

You can never go any higher than your thinking.

BENJAMIN DISRAELI

Seize every new, exciting opportunity

You probably first began to notice a need for something in your life to change because of a sense of unease deep inside. Perhaps something started niggling you, telling you over and over that life was not as good as it should be. Maybe you were unhappy in your job, or your relationship wasn't working. Perhaps your business wasn't going the way you wanted. Or you felt unfulfilled – could it be that you were simply bored?

So why is it that, despite such change often being seen as highly desirable, actually bringing it about can seem something of a challenge? What is it that might be stopping you from following through on your intentions on a much bigger scale than you have previously allowed? How do you break through to bigger, more exciting goals? Big audacious goals that stand in front of you and yell, 'Take me – if you dare!'

Push your boundaries

In this tactic we are going to explore ways to open up your thinking and being, so as to bring about two significant developments. On the one hand, you will discover a step-by-step process that will help you embrace change rather than fear it. On the other hand, you may start to feel increasingly that you want to expand your thinking into new areas of possibility and even foster a burning desire to step into uncharted territory. You may want to push your boundaries and explore just how far you could go.

Most people are not willing to do whatever it takes to reach their next level. They might talk a lot about their dreams and desires, but taking serious action towards them demands more than a passing interest. It demands commitment. Commitment is something you can create and control. What's more, you will find that, as you build on and power up your commitment to change, so you will become a different person – a person with fire in their belly and passion for life. Then, as you become aware of new opportunities, you'll be able to zone in on them with a laser-like focus, ready to live them for real.

Small steps work

Most change happens in small, incremental steps. Even tiny steps, repeated daily, can lead to very significant outcomes over time. Imagine if an aircraft were to take off from Los Angeles and fly to London in a straight line. The pilot would identify a course to set and follow that course. If he were to change the course by just one degree, the ultimate destination of the aircraft would be very different. The same is true in life, in business, in love ... A small change in the course you set can bring about a completely different destination. It's the small actions repeated frequently that bring about results, the small actions going in the direction you've chosen.

Think of a time in the past when you created a change in your life that wasn't too difficult to put into practice. You probably launched into it quite quickly, simply because it wasn't too difficult to do and you could see the benefits or rewards quite clearly. It may be that you decided to cut down on your sugar intake, or started associating more with people whose company you found more stimulating and rewarding, or perhaps you decided to save up for something special. You are no stranger to bringing about change. You have done it many times before. You already have the basic skills required. What we'll do now is sharpen up those skills to create a powerful tool for you to use whenever you decide that you want your life to be noticeably different in some way, and are ready to commit to making it happen.

Live with outrageous passion

You may have come to the point in your life when you find it no longer acceptable to maintain the status quo, to lead an ordinary existence. You may have come to believe that you are ready to inject your life with a new vitality, to grab your opportunities fiercely with both hands and be taken on a wild, adventurous journey. Doing nothing is no longer an option. You may have come to realize that, every day, we are either growing or dying. We are either moving forward or slipping backwards. Nothing is static. There is no middle ground. The composer Stravinsky is reported to have made this remark about musicians: 'If you miss a day's practice, you notice it. If you miss two days' practice, your enemies notice it. If you miss three days, your friends notice.' This insight is not the preserve of musicians. It applies to every aspect of human endeavour. You have the power to bring about radical change in your life through small improvements in your performance applied every day – and people will certainly begin to notice the new swagger in your step as you experience growing levels of success.

Another person might say, 'Thank you, I'm comfortable.' However, that's not you. Isn't it more likely that, by now, you are becoming increasingly conscious of a newly evolved sense of purpose that has been lying quietly dormant within you? This is a drive that is now ready to emerge, to stretch your limits and to explore more of the potential that is clamouring to unleash itself on the world around you.

Rick Snyder, professor of clinical psychology at the University of Kansas, has done a number of studies concerning the thinking of outstanding achievers. He identified five personal characteristics common to top performers:

- Ability to find motivation from within themselves.
- Resourcefulness to find the means of accomplishing what they want.
- Strength of spirit to overcome difficulties that may arise.
- Flexibility to find different ways of achieving their goals – or to switch goals if one becomes impossible.
- Ability to break down large tasks into smaller, manageable chunks.

As you become aware of these resources, you can train yourself to raise your performance in each one. By applying them in your daily life, you can't help but bring about bigger, more rewarding outcomes. Create a scorecard in your journal and, at the end of each month, give yourself a score out of ten for how well you have done in each. Then decide what you are going to do over the next month to raise the bar a little. (You will find a prepared scorecard and goal-accelerator chart in the members' area of www.tactics4talent.com.)

It's impossible to repress excellence of thinking; the elite can't be held back. Leadership thinking built on sound foundations always emerges at the front and, as we know, thoughts lead to actions ...

Be passionate about growing your future. Here's the secret. There are just two reasons why people fail to achieve their potential. Either they don't know what to do, or they can't find the motivation to do what they need to do. That's it! The rest are details. When you understand this fundamental, you will find yourself well placed to shift your outcomes to a whole new level. Which of these two factors might be holding you back? What will you do about it? Who could help you achieve what you want?

Now that you have come so far, it's time to raise the stakes. Take a close look at where you are now. What inspires you about your new potential? When are you going to start planning your next adventure? Is there room to grow some more, no matter what your age or circumstances? What might you need to do to bring in new life energy?

Christopher Howard, the author of *Instant Wealth: Wake Up Rich!* and an influential trainer in personal excellence, often speaks of 'ferocious curiosity'. This is a powerful commodity for super-achievers. What if ...? Just suppose ... How would it be if ...? Just because something seems impossible or ridiculous right now doesn't mean it will always be so. Today, it's very difficult to imagine life without the internet, for instance. Yet, if you had mentioned to someone fifty years ago the possibility of connecting with people from all over the world from a screen in your own home, they would probably have smiled benignly and thought you had lost the plot.

Be willing to push the bounds of your imagination: it's your future you are creating.

Vertical change

Change need not necessarily be a change in direction. Often it's more about making a shift in your level of performance. You may feel comfortable in what you are doing, but are simply developing a feeling that you've been

TACTICS IN ACTION

The 'eureka' moment

Philippe Petit was idly flipping through a magazine when his eye stopped at a page describing how two towers were being built on the southernmost tip of Manhattan Island in New York. The year was 1968 and the plan was to build the tallest towers in the USA – a monument to human achievement, vision and modern engineering. A shiver ran down Philippe's spine. This was a pivotal moment in his life. There and then he knew that he would have to take a walk between the two towers – a quarter of a mile above Manhattan – on a tightrope.

Before he was twenty years old Philippe had trained himself to be a wire-walker, constantly pushing his boundaries – the forward somersault, the backward somersault, the unicycle … none of it was enough. He discarded these 'tricks' and proceeded, as he put it, 'to reinvent my art'.

The Twin Towers 'coup' took him to a whole new dimension. Once the seed of the idea was planted, there was no going back for him. He became passionately focused on his outrageous project.

Petit and his accomplices spent six years planning every last detail in preparation. They studied the effects the wind would have on the swaying buildings. They disguised themselves as construction workers to slip into the buildings unnoticed so they could do their research. Philippe passed himself off as a journalist sent to interview the workers to get access to the roof.

On 6 August 1974, Philippe and his crew rode, with all their equipment, in an elevator up to the 104th floor of the south tower. They used a bow and arrow to shoot a line from one building to the other, first using fishing line and then increasingly thicker ropes until they were able to affix a 204-kg (450-lb) steel cable between the two towers.

Soon after 7.15 am, Philippe stepped out onto the wire, balancing pole in his hands, while people 110 storeys below watched spellbound. For forty-five minutes he walked, he ran, he danced, he bounced, he lay on the wire, he laughed … The sheer exquisite beauty of the performance, for performer and audience alike, was unparalleled.

On that morning his dream had come to life and nothing could be the same again. When asked about it, he simply said, 'When I see three oranges, I juggle; when I see two towers, I walk.'

playing too small. Is it now time to push your boundaries further, to take on new challenges in your field that will inspire you and help you grow into a bigger person? Sometimes a single catalytic moment can trigger a new way of thinking. It may simply be something that someone says, or a phrase that catches your eye and fires up your imagination. By increasingly becoming a person who is open to the adventures that life can bring (even if it does mean stepping into the unknown at times), you make yourself more attuned to the world of possibility created by new ideas. If you feel that the ideas are slow in coming, use the four-step exercise on pages 147–8 to ask yourself how you could raise your game.

What would it take to shock you?

I was in the marina in Antibes on the south coast of France, arguably one of the most glamorous and spectacular marinas in the world, indulging my passion for sailing and all things nautical. Call it eye candy on an epic scale, if you like. Each yacht was more stunningly beautiful than the last. Each had her own story of magnificence and adventure. This is very much a place where no expense is spared in the pursuit of excellence. Every last detail has had thought, vision and love lavished on it, whether on the craft itself or the voyages to far-flung parts of the world that the owner and crew might undertake.

Suddenly, a vessel sailed in that was even more impressive than the others. Her crew, immaculately turned out in red polo shirts and smart beige shorts, skilfully manoeuvred her into her berth. I casually remarked to the friend I was with that if I were captain of this yacht, taking her out for the first time, I'd be terrified of bumping into something. The cost of such a craft is colossal, and the sheer indignity of such an episode would be mortifying.

No sooner had I uttered those words than I felt like an arrow of cold steel had penetrated me deep inside. I was shocked to the core. It was as if I had touched a raw nerve. As I heard myself speak I realized that, until that time,

▶ PAGE 149

EXERCISE **THE FOUR-STEP EXERCISE**

This powerful four-step process is based on research by David Kolb at the University of Cleveland, Ohio, which was later developed further by Dr Bernice McCarthy. It breaks down into manageable chunks how we, as human beings, learn from our experiences. It creates an openness of mind to new possibilities and by focusing on each stage in turn you will ask yourself questions that will build a strong framework for the change that you would like to see happening in your life. It's a system that is now widely used throughout the world in business and government for accelerated learning.

Set aside some time to be in a quiet, comfortable environment, somewhere you feel relaxed and at peace with yourself and with the world. You may like to have some soothing music playing in the background (baroque music works well for this exercise) or simply enjoy the sounds of nature around you.

Take a few minutes just to concentrate on your breathing and empty your mind of thoughts.

When you are quietly settled, let your mind take some time to address each one of the questions that follows on the next page in turn. As you explore your thoughts, write down what you are thinking in your journal or on a piece of paper. Avoid any judgmental thoughts. Just write what is, what you notice.

Remember, when you write, you let your unconscious mind speak. Who knows what you might discover ...

▶ PAGE 148

Step 1:

Why do I want this to change?

How would my life be different if things changed?

What would I like to be experiencing?

How would my life be different if things changed?

Step 2:

What exactly is it that needs to change?

What could happen if I decided ...?

What would happen if I chose to maintain the status quo?

How might I feel if I started to change this?

Step 3:

How would it look if I raised my game by just 1 per cent tomorrow?

How can I simplify what I need to do?

What one thing could I do right now to bring change into my life?

What one thing would I be willing to commit to doing right now?

Step 4:

What could happen if I raised my game by 1 per cent every day?

What could happen if I dared to dream a bigger dream?

What could happen if I lived up to who I was born to be?

What could happen if I allowed the genius within me to awake?

I had been thinking purely in terms of yachts I could probably afford (possibly with a small 'margin for error').

I asked myself whether that would be the level of thinking that the captain of the yacht we were admiring, or her owner, would have entertained. What would be the mindset of someone commissioning a vessel like this, their vision, their aspiration? I wondered how it would feel to set foot on 'my new yacht' for the first time. The thoughts flowed fast and furious.

In those few moments I learned how much more I still needed to grow and change. I discovered how much I still needed to expand my thinking and the horizons of my vision. My mind went into overdrive. 'What are the new questions I am going to need to ask myself? Who are the new people I need to connect with? What is it that needs to change within me?'

It's not that right now I want or need a 55-m (180-ft) yacht and crew to operate her. Nor do I need the financial resources that were clearly behind this exquisite boat. No, it was something more fundamental. It was the realization that in those few moments I had triggered a new stage in my journey of growth. It was time to take action.

The billionaire's signature

I remember T. Harv Eker, author of *Secrets of the Millionaire Mind*, once saying, 'When I became a millionaire, even my signature changed. When I became a billionaire, it changed again.' Our signature is something very personal. It's a reflection of who we are. As you change and grow, and as you reach for new peaks of achievement, you will also find that your signature changes. You will be evolving into a reinvented you.

You will find yourself with the courage to look for and embrace a new way of being. You will find your life taking on a new level of meaning and purpose. You will experience an inner need to break down barriers and explore the potential that life has to offer to those who are willing to challenge the status quo. You will find yourself showing up in the world as a person of new significance and influence. You will find yourself living with passion!

TACTICS

WHAT NEXT?

The future belongs to people who see possibilities
before they become obvious.

TED LEVITT

Your journey forward

Can you imagine the day when you look around you, consider what you do every day, what you feel every day, what you have achieved, and you exclaim to yourself, 'What an amazing life!'?

When the time does come to say it, you will also know two things. One: you have arrived there because of the actions that you took. Two: those actions were possible because of thoughts that you had. You designed and created your life.

You will also be aware that you are on the launch pad for even greater success because once you have established within yourself the ways of thinking and doing things of an elite performer, your momentum will become very powerful indeed.

What's changed?

We have covered a lot of ground in our work together. We have looked at what is important to you and why. We have considered the sort of person you need to become in order to achieve who you want to be. We have confronted fears and obstacles that held you back from doing what you most want to do. We have seen how what you do and the way you interact with other people impacts on what you can make possible, both for others and for yourself.

As you worked through the exercises and thought around the questions we have discussed, you may have gradually noticed something changing. You are not the same person you were when we began our journey together. You have become more aware of the rich potential that lies ahead of you. You have awakened within yourself a curiosity for what else might be possible. You have begun an extraordinary journey of personal growth and achievement. Yet this is still just the beginning.

When you start to become more curious about what might be possible, you will find that curiosity increasing even more as time goes by. It's part of

▶ PAGE 154

EXERCISE **TAKE YOUR OWN ADVICE**

We all like to think we're adept at giving advice to other people. Sometimes, though, it feels good to receive advice from someone who is knowledgeable and wise. When you are in the middle of an issue, it can be difficult to see everything as it really is, so it's valuable to have an outside opinion.

In our work together you have accumulated a great deal of knowledge. Because of this, if your best friend were to need some advice, you are now perfectly equipped to help them. Similarly, if your best friend had done all the developmental work that you have, you would no doubt value their wisdom and support. Look back over the ground we have covered and start to bring the strands together. Notice what has changed for you. How are you thinking differently? What are you doing differently? How has your understanding of the processes for success grown?

It's part of human nature to be much more resourceful when we are trying to help other people than when we look at our own situation. Use this exercise to obtain for yourself the maximum value from what you have learned.

1.   Identify a challenge you are currently wrestling with and on which you would like an opinion. Make sure you can articulate clearly where you would like advice, and make sure you have all your facts straight before you ask.

2.   Go somewhere where you and your 'friend' could have a private conversation, undisturbed.

3.   Sit down and imagine your friend is sitting there with you. Proceed to describe the challenge that you face and the help that you would like. Make your friend's presence as vivid as possible – play out the scene as if they were really present. Go all out for it and make it as real as possible.

4. When you think your friend has the full picture, move over into their seat and become the friend you were talking to. Think yourself into their persona; detach yourself from who you were a moment ago.

5. You can now respond as your friend: 'That's interesting. As I understand it …' and proceed to outline what you have just heard. Then draw on all your accumulated wisdom and give your advice from your point of view: what else might be possible, what other approaches could be explored, who might have additional knowledge to share, and so on. Take your time. Draw on the full extent of your accumulated wisdom. Be supportive to your friend. You have their best interests at heart.

6. Now move back over to your original seat and respond as the real you. 'Ah! So you think …' and repeat what you have just heard yourself say. At the end of your response, thank your friend for their help and support.

This is a remarkably simple exercise, but it's astonishingly effective. When you really play each part full out, the process will bring extraordinary clarity of thinking to the challenge facing you.

Another way to do it is with a real live friend. You explain the issue at hand; your friend repeats it word for word to you. You then proceed to give your friend advice based on what they have said to you – and of course take in the full extent of the advice you are actually giving yourself. It can be just as effective.

our natural human condition to want to grow – so let go, and allow yourself to become even more who you really are.

As we noted at the start of **Tactic 10,** the former British Prime Minister Benjamin Disraeli once observed, 'You can never go any higher than your thinking.' You know that it's important for you to keep pushing the boundaries of your imagination. Keep exploring what else might be possible. Also, remember to celebrate your achievements, because it's important to acknowledge that they are something YOU have made possible and done. Were it not for the thoughts you'd had and the actions you'd taken, they would not have happened.

Then ask yourself the question, 'Is there an even better way of doing things?' What if you were to approach your life from an even more expanded sense of awareness? What if someone more creative and visionary than you were looking at this? What if you were to perform at an even higher level?

Make it possible

As you now know, success is not going to happen by accident or wishful thinking. Your task is to go out into the world and make it happen. Live the life you really want to live. Make sure that what you do every day is in line with what's really important to you and to your values. Associate with people who are already living the life that you want to be living. Read books, visit websites and attend seminars that will expand your vision and empower you to ask what more is possible. Build on your skills and the quality of the influences with which you surround yourself so that you continue to grow. Play full out in your mastermind group – the people you have assembled around you who are all committed to delivering as elite performers – and let the other members challenge your assumptions. Perhaps hire a good personal coach to help you arrive where you need to be, faster and more effectively than you could get there on your own.

Invest your time, your thinking and your resources in yourself, because you are the best and most reliable investment that you could possibly make. It's through what you do that you will achieve the best returns on that investment.

Lance Armstrong, the cyclist and winner of the Tour de France seven consecutive times, says, 'There's a point in every race when a rider encounters his real opponent and understands that it's himself.'

It's when you consciously break through the barriers in your own mind that you create the platform to reach new levels of achievement. Sometimes it can be tempting to underestimate the extent of your true potential and consequently settle for less. However, you now have the inner strength and confidence to know that you deserve more. Focus on the passionate pursuit of excellence and on what could be. Be willing to do whatever it takes and sculpt for yourself a life that is significant, a life that is truly world class.

The reason why

Make it your business to see that, when you come to your final hour, as we all will one day, you can look back on a life lived to the full. Make sure you can look back with delight at what you did, at what you achieved, at what you made happen. But remember, as you come to your last moments, you will not be poring over your bank statements, looking with pride at the luxury car in your drive or organizing your next celebration party. What will be much more important to you will be the legacy that you leave behind. How did you change the world? How many lives did you touch and inspire? How many people did you help? Each one of us is here for a reason, and I believe that reason is to make a difference in the world. It's when we live up to that reason that we experience the feelings of fulfilment, inner joy and happiness that we as human beings all crave. Step up to your edge and let your life count for all it can.

Do what others say cannot be done. Be who others say you cannot be. Listen to what your heart says, and act on what you hear. Do what you must do with unbridled passion; do it so hard that the surprise of it takes even YOUR breath away. You were born to perform at world class. Do it!

A final word

An extraordinary life is something that you create. Remember, it's not something that you do once and then sit back and watch unfold. It is something you work at each day. As you do so, your success will accelerate and you will find yourself building a remarkable future. Think of it in physical terms. When you work out in the gym regularly and eat appropriately, you reap the rewards. Your body takes on shape; you become fitter, healthier, and you feel much better within yourself, too.

In the same way, use what you have learned in this book as the foundation for your future growth. Play full out every day. Do whatever it takes. Develop a burning desire constantly to know more and to explore new possibilities. Use the resources opposite and at www.tactics4talent.com to help you on your journey.

Resources

Books

Adrienne, Carol and Redfield, James. *The Celestine Prophecy: An Experiential Guide*. London: Bantam, 1995

Barefoot Doctor. *Urban Warrior*. London: Piatkus Books, 1998

Branson, Richard. *Losing My Virginity*. London: Virgin Books, 2007

Branson, Richard. *Business Stripped Bare: Adventures of a Global Entrepreneur*. London: Random House, 2008

Bronson, Po. *What Should I Do with My Life?* London: Secker & Warburg, 2003

Bungay Stanier, Michael. *Do More Great Work*. New York: Workman, 2010

Canfield, Jack. *The Success Principles*. London: HarperCollins, 2005

Canfield, Jack, Hansen, Mark Victor and Hewitt, Les. *The Power of Focus*. Deerfield Beach, FL: Health Communications, 2000

Chopra, Deepak. *The Seven Spiritual Laws of Success*. London: Random House, 1996

Cialdini, Robert B. *Influence*. New York: HarperCollins, 2007

Cohen, Alan. *Relax into Wealth*. London: Piatkus Books, 2007

Comaford-Lynch, Christine. *Rules for Renegades*. New York: McGraw-Hill, 2007

Dyer, Dr Wayne W. *Inspiration*. Carlsbad, CA: Hay House, 2006

Dyer, Dr Wayne W. *Stop the Excuses*. London: Hay House, 2009

Eker, T. Harv. *Secrets of the Millionaire Mind*. New York: HarperCollins, 2005

Fried, Jason and Hansson, Heinemeier David. *Rework*. London: Random House, 2010

Goleman, Daniel. *Emotional Intelligence*. London: Bloomsbury, 1996

Hansen, Mark Victor and Allen, Robert G. *The One Minute Millionaire*. London: Random House, 2002

Hansen, Mark Victor and Allen, Robert G. *Cracking the Millionaire Code*. London: Random House, 2005

Hardy, Darren. *The Compound Effect*. Dallas: Success Books, 2010

Hill, Napoleon. *Think and Grow Rich*. New York: Random House, 1988

Holden, Robert. *Success Intelligence*. London: Hodder & Stoughton, 2005

Howard, Christopher. *Instant Wealth – Wake Up Rich!* Hoboken, NJ: John Wiley, 2010

Johnson, Spencer. *Who Moved My Cheese?* London: Random House, 1999

Kiyosaki, Robert T. *Rich Dad Poor Dad*. New York: Warner Books, 2000

Leighton, Allan. *On Leadership*. London: Random House, 2007

Malhotra, Deepak and Bazerman, Max H. *Negotiation Genius*, New York: Bantam Dell, 2007

Mapes, James. *Quantum Leap Thinking*. London: Souvenir Press, 2001

Martin, Patricia. *RenGen: Renaissance Generation*. Avon, MA: F & W Publications, 2007

Martin, Roger L. *The Opposable Mind: How Successful Leaders Win Through Integrative Thinking*. Boston: Harvard Business School Press, 2007

McKenna, Paul. *Instant Confidence*. London: Random House, 2006

Schwartz, David J. *The Magic of Thinking Big*. London: Simon & Schuster, 1995

Sharma, Robin. *Discover Your Destiny*. London: HarperCollins, 2004

Sharma, Robin. *The Greatness Guide*. London: HarperCollins, 2006

Sharma, Robin. *The Leader Who Had No Title*. New York: Simon & Schuster, 2010

Sharma, Robin. *The Monk Who Sold His Ferrari*. London: HarperCollins, 2004

Sieger, Robin. *Natural Born Winners*. London: Random House, 2004

Smith, Paul. *How to Have an Outstanding Life*. Sydney: New Holland, 2005

Taylor, David. *The Naked Leader*. London: Bantam, 2003

Templar, Richard. *The Rules of Wealth*. Harlow: Pearson Education, 2007

Thurston Hurst, Kenneth. *Live Life First Class*. New York: Samuel Weiser, 1985

Todd, Michael. *The Twelve Conditions of a Miracle*. New York: Penguin, 2004

Tolle, Eckhart. *A New Earth*. London: Penguin, 2009

Tolle, Eckhart. *Practising the Power of Now*. London: Hodder & Stoughton, 2001

Williams, Nick. *The Work We Were Born To Do*. London: HarperCollins, 1999

Williams, Nick. *Unconditional Success*. London: Random House, 2003

Wiseman, Prof. Richard. *59 Seconds: Think a Little, Change a Lot*. London: Macmillan, 2009

Note: The author has made every effort to contact where appropriate the copyright owners of the extracts used in this book, and invites those who may not have responded to contact him via the publisher.

Websites

www.achievement.org
www.robinsharma.com
www.success.com
www.thecompoundeffect.com
www.wealthandachievement.com

More links and recommendations are being added every day to the members' area of www.tactics4talent.com.

The author

Jan Zuchowski is an inspirational trainer and coach, and an expert in business psychology and communication skills. Jan originally trained as a classical musician and worked as a choral director, performing in the UK and around Europe. From this teaching and training experience he developed a fascination and passion for the psychology of personal achievement. Initially he worked with musicians, successfully helping them realize their creative and performance potential. As the effectiveness of his training for super-achievement through mindset building became recognized, his reputation spread and he adapted his techniques in other fields – first with sportspeople, notably in the field of competition sailing, and then with executives in the business environment.

Jan is described as a high-impact business strategist and trainer in business leadership, and a specialist in mind process re-engineering. He is continually researching and assessing the latest and most effective thinking in psychology as it can be applied to personal performance. He has drawn influence in his work from such luminaries as Robert G. Allen, Richard Bandler, Wayne Dyer, T. Harv Eker, Christopher Howard and Robin Sharma.

Jan lives in London and travels regularly to the US, working with both corporate and private clients to help them explore the full extent of their potential and to perform at a world-class level.

Be the change you wish to see.

Mahatma Gandhi

Acknowledgements

I offer my deepest gratitude and thanks to all who have so kindly and generously helped in the creation of this book:

To Hal Robinson, a fantastic editor and wise and insightful friend, who not only made the project possible, but was my guiding light and mentor throughout; to Nick Eddison and Ian Jackson at Eddison Sadd for their vision and belief in me and in what could be possible; to Katie Golsby and Ali Moore, my brilliant editors, and to all the team at Eddison Sadd for all their hard work; to Simon Banks, Sally Eden and Michele Wilke for their help with stories and suggestions; to the following people who have directly helped me shape my own success and achievements through their seminars, workshops and coaching programmes: Robert G. Allan, Duane Alley, Richard Bandler, Dr Wayne Dyer, T. Harv Eker, Christopher Howard, Paul McKenna and Robin Sharma; to all my fellow authors from whose writings I have had the privilege to be able to quote; to my friends at Librios for all the help with the website that accompanies the book and training programmes; and to all my family and friends who gave me so much support and encouragement in my writing.

Thank you all for making this project possible!

EDDISON•SADD EDITIONS
Concept Nick Eddison
Mac Designer Brazzle Atkins
Editorial Director Ian Jackson
Editors Katie Golsby and Ali Moore
Proofreader Nikky Twyman
Production Sarah Rooney

Arrow illustration: iStockphoto/Palto; photography by Brazzle Atkins